# RED SQUARE,
# BLACK SQUARE

Suny Series, The Margins of Literature
Mihai I. Spariosu, editor

# RED SQUARE, BLACK SQUARE

# RED SQUARE, BLACK SQUARE

## Organon for Revolutionary Imagination

by
Vladislav Todorov

State University of New York Press

Published by
State University of New York Press, Albany



For information, address the State University of New York Press,
State University Plaza, Albany, NY 12246

Library of Congress Cataloging-in-Publication Data

Todorov, Vladislav.
    Red square, black square : organon for revolutionary imagination /
by Vladislav Todorov.
       p.   cm.—(SUNY series, the margins of literature)
    Includes bibliographical references.
    ISBN 0-7914-2191-0 (alk. paper). —ISBN 0-7914-2192-9 (pbk. :
alk. paper)
     1. Russian literature—20th century—History and criticism.
  2. Modernism (Literature)—Soviet Union.   3. Art, Russian.
  4. Modernism (Art)—Soviet Union.   5. Communist aesthetics.
  I. Title.   II. Series.
  PG3020.5.M6T63   1995
  891.709′358—dc20                                                          93-47101
                                                                                  CIP

10 9 8 7 6 5 4 3 2 1

to B. and to B.

# Contents

Imagine Horatio possessed by the secret drive to have the corpse of Hamlet mummified.

## The QUESTion: Who to be?

Fortinbras—the leader of the conquest, or, Horatio—the guide through the ruined space? The one who sweeps out the ruins or the one who collects and assembles them into shocking figures? The one who writes new just laws or the one who reads the rough face of the ruins thus extracting the grand narrative of the past?

That is the QUEST-ion!

These are the two missions for the Intellect witnessing the end of the system. Horatio is my guide. He is my Virgil initiating me into the infernal space.

## The Collector

The Collector is a major figure in Benjamin's works. Poisoned by melancholy his imagination gets excited when touching the contagious matter of the remnants. He spends his time in his (al-) political laboratory mixing substances of the past, contemplating the reactions, elaborating his craft to embalm and stuff the body of history and to derive specters out of it. The grand ruin is the ugly embryo of paranoid visions. It bears specters into life.

The act of reading ruins and fractured objects needs some deliberately twisted linguistic devices that figuratively resemble the ruined space itself. This book goes even further, it endeavors to materialize a paradox—to build up a wreckage.

The philosopher as a (re)collector of ruins inhabits the end.

## The Physio-Gnomic Style

### HIPPOCRATIC FACE

*The signs to watch for in acute diseases are as follows.
First study the patient's face . . . the more abnormal it
is, the worse it is. The terminal appearance may be described thus: sharp nose, sunken eyes, the temples fallen
in, the ears cold and retracted with distorted lobes, the*

*skin of the face hard, stretched and dry, and the color of
the face pale and dusky . . . and if there is no improvement within the prescribed time, it must be realized that
this sign portends death.*
> Hippocrates, "Prognosis," no. 2

*Physio-gnomic* is the mode of reading wreaked objects and faces. *Gnomic* is the style of this book. The original meaning of *Physio-gnomonica* is to acquire knowledge of the virtual condition of a human being by discerning its appearance, by reading its face as a configuration of features and expressions: *physis* is the system of nature and *gnome* is judgment of a special kind. *Gnome* is a short, aphoristic statement or maxim that formulates the nature of being.

The ancient physician Hippocrates teaches how one may read the symptoms of a disease through the changing complexion and recognize the advent of death by the contortion features. The face is recognized as a battlefield where a lethal *agon* is staged. The face is at once the stage and the performer of the agony between life and death. As living nature dies in the features of the face it is transformed from an arena into a cemetery.

In ancient times a mask was laid upon the face of the corpse in order to seal the physiognomy for eternity. The death-mask is the ultimate sclerosis of the face. It is an allegorical device assembled of ruins. This mask pieces the ruins of life together into an icon. The mask appropriates the physiognomy of the corpse and shifts it beyond decay. As the so-called Hippocratic face is an aphorism of death, it must be written down in another medium, more solid than mere flesh, for the corporeal graph of the face is subject to decay. Death impregnates the face with decay. The mask solidifies it for eternity.

### THE DREAMS OF A CORPSE

*The key-figure of the early allegory is the corpse. The
key-figure of the later allegory is the "souvenir."*
> Benjamin, "Central Park," no. 44

Imagine the Lenin mummy as a lurid *gnomon* that casts the shadow of communism on the face of the earth. Hence, a *physio-gnomonic* mode of writing will embrace it as its cult instrument.

When communism set foot in the world, it molded a physiognomic space of its own. It unfolded a grand monumental exterior fortified with the gross faces of the teachers and stuffed with aphorisms of the doctrine. Although justified by science, pre-planned and pre-rationalized, communism had to be enforced by allegorical devices—images, visions, ceremonies and monuments. The Corpse—the mummy of the Leader— pins down the center of this gigantic exterior. The Corpse unfolds the physiognomic spaces of communism. It induces universal melancholy and organizes people's mass grief. The Corpse is the engine of the people's paranoia. The mummy is the incarnate of the roaming communist specter which advertises its own imaginary space. If the teaching of the leader is the rational motive of communism, his Corpse is the carnal one. Thus communism merges the rational and the carnal in a political mode of life. The mummy suggests a politicized melancholy.

The Corpse of Lenin has no Hippocratic face, no physiognomy to be decoded. Not death but dreams inhabit its face. For the face of the Corpse is as if alive, sleeping and dreaming: and its dreams are the lives of the people. The corpse dreams life. The corpse dreams us and we become its nightmare. Our lives are its politically justified paranoia. The Communist state is the set for the corpse's dream. Science and paranoia, rational and absurd are radically united in the Corpse. There is nothing beyond it. Here is life and life is grieving. In the works of Platonov grief is the psychic mode, much as horror in the works of Kafka.

Whatever terror it unleashes, communism is excused, for a corpse may have nightmares. What overcomes the terror is people's existential sympathy for the poor Corpse suffering nightmares. Mourning, melancholy, paranoia—this is the mood around a Corpse dreaming communism.


## THE PRINCIPLE OF ORNAMENTAL MANNERISM

*Of course the script should not be a simple one; it's not supposed to kill straight off but at an average of twelve hours; the turning point is reckoned to come at the sixth hour. So there have to be lots and lots of ornaments around the original script; the script itself runs around the body only in a narrow girdle; the rest of the body is reserved for the ornamentation. Can you appreciate now the work of the harrow and the whole apparatus?—Just watch it!*

*Kafka, "The Penal Colony"*

Just watch it!

*Fragmentation* is the principle of this book.

The fragmentation should be perceived as a precise intervention that causes a miniature fracture and cuts to the very quick of the bone structure. A fragment demonstrates the point and the design much more graphically than anything else could possibly do, either the logical or the rhetorical skeleton of this book. The fragment ultimately magnifies the point and provokes vision. What should be understood should be beheld.

*The fragment: this is the noblest matter of Baroque creation.*
> W. Benjamin, *Origin of the German Trauerspiel*

*Aphorism* is the bond of this book.

Aphorism radically unites theoretical observation, experimental operation and rhetorical dress.

Think of the aphorism as a modernized dithyramb! For it bonds theory, practice and utterance within an ornament—a miniature oratory.

Aphorism is a special case of oration, incantation—an elevating and demonstrative staging of the issue. Aphorism is theatricalized theory. It reverts theory back to the theater, observation to ceremonial beholding, sight to insight. Aphorism molds the physiognomy of the issue.

When a sharp vision impregnates the word, it proliferates ornaments through it. Ornaments testify to the conception of the ideas in the physiology of language. This book is a compound ornament.

*Ornamental mannerism* is the style of the book. Dithyramb, gnome, aphorism are the ancient, original forms of ornamental mannerism. This is a deliberate and demonstrative way to compose sentences that makes every single word in this book and the entity of the book itself something built on purpose. The whole enterprise implements a premeditated design: to manufacture a suggestive narrative that will bring the grand past back in the aggregated wreckage of the present. Words descend on the harsh sur-face of a wrecked reality and imprint its relief upon themselves.

The book itself creates what sustains it. The ship itself creates the sea it sails.

## The Ornament Under Modernism

### THE ARRESTED ORNAMENT

*The modern man who tattoos himself is either a criminal*
*or degenerate. There are prisons in which eighty per*
*cent of the inmates show tattoos. The tattooed who are*
*not in prison are latent criminals or degenerate aristo-*

*crats. If someone who is tattooed dies at liberty, it means
he has died a few years before committing a murder.*

*The urge to ornament one's face and everything
within reach is the start of plastic art. It is the baby talk
of painting. All art is erotic.*

*The first ornament that was born, the cross, was
erotic in origin. The first work of art, the first artistic
act which the first artist, in order to rid himself of his
surplus energy, smeared on the wall. A horizontal dash:
the prone woman. A vertical dash: the man penetrating
her. The man who created it felt the same urge as
Beethoven, he was in the same heaven in which
Beethoven created the Ninth Symphony.*

*But the man of our day who, in response to an in-
ner urge, smears the walls with erotic symbols is a criminal or a degenerate. It goes without saying that this
impulse most frequently assails people with such symptoms of degeneracy in the lavatory.*

*I have made the following discovery and I pass it
on to the world: The evolution of culture is synonymous
with the removal of ornament from utilitarian objects.*

*Adolph Loos, "Ornament and Crime"*
*(in Conrads 1970, 19)*

## MODERNISM ONCE AGAIN

*The real world . . . has always been the apparent world
once again.*

*Nietzsche, The Will to Power, 566*

The grand object of postmodernism is the project of modernism staged demonstratively once again. I would argue that modernism has no end in itself. Its end perpetually recedes before us (in the future). Completion of modernism is that same modernism once again. Precisely the postmodern endeavor stages the end. Thus it frames modernism.

I could establish a causal relation between modernism and postmodernism only on the basis of a paradox: the paradox of the self-portrait. While painting a self-portrait the artist gradually vanishes into it. And the brush, this indispensable prosthesis of creation remains attached to the work as the final stroke. Thus a rose remained completely (completed) in its name.

The postmodern mode makes you an actor standing at the end—an actor who holds in his hands the already proclaimed end(s) of history, art, ideology, God and so forth. The actor pulls these ends and thus he turns the gigantic body of culture into a formidable marionette. The better you master the ends, the more organs and members of this body you will activate and the more stunning its movement becomes.

There is no way to escape from the bond of civilization you were raised in. Better drag it, this is your link to the body you want to shake up. My bond was called "communism." I consider it the last existing political installation of the modernist project that collapsed. The revolutionary project for building an unprecedented society utterly expressed the radical left modernism. The work of art happened to be used as a special kind of laboratory for designing and testing the project. Thus political and aesthetic dimentions merged into one vision. Then came the rigid period of a total party enforcement of the vision and authorization of the project—the Red doctrine and the proletarian dictatorship. Communism petrified modernism. Lenin was mummified and this marked the beginning of the rigid stage. I regard the mummy as the most astonishing end of modernism. Then the vision feverishly consumed the entire social reality. Thus came my own endeavor to grasp this end.

I conceive my work as an action performed with the sclerotic end of the communist endeavor. I perform with the end(s) of the doctrine. And the "ornamental mannerism," as I name the style manifested throughout the book, comes to expose my aesthetic attitude toward the deadends of modernism.

The problem is how to tackle this specific end of history. How to pull it off in writing? How to retrieve the initial arbitrariness of the modernist discourse and thus suspend its political self-authorization and drain everything away but its artistic impulse to mold a total space?

If you can imagine the double face of Janus as a temporal figure, you will get my point. This side that faces the future is a rigid mask. The living one mirrors the past.

# Beginning

Communism is not impending. It has already happened.

Communism created ultimately effective aesthetic structures and ultimately defective economic ones. That is what empowers its strong presence and durability in the world. That is what fortifies it.

Factories are not built to produce commodities. They produce the united-working-class-body. They are allegorical figures of industrialization. Industry represents the leading metaphor of party ideology and factories are the works of this ideology. They result in a deficit of goods, but an overproduction of symbolic meanings. Their essence is aesthetic, not economic. They are the poems of communist ideology. The work process creates just these factories-poems, not commodities. Labor is a ceremony begetting the communal body of the working class. The worker labors for the sake of the factory-poem, not for the sake of the market. The aim of labor in the factory is the poetic completeness of the factory itself.

*Promyshlennost'* in Russian means industry. Originally the word designated an entire order of things that has been completely thought out. It is a derivative form of *myslit'*—to think; *myshlenie*—thinking; *mysl'*—thought. It is a verbal noun with a prefix *pro-* that implies a going through, or making thoroughly, penetrating throughout. The Old Church Slavonic meaning of *pro-mysl* is pro-vidence and indicates the Divine thought of the Lord that thoroughly pervades the entirety of the world. Hence *promyshlennost'* (industry) suggests a major realm of the social life that has been thoroughly thought out and is pervaded by a supreme Intelligence that pro-vides its perfection of an unique piece of genius. It would be a realm that was pre-viewed by a powerful Reason, projected and supervised by the ubiquitous vision of a Master.

Communism reified precisely this sacred meaning of the word by establishing One-party-plan-industry. It is a zone of reality where Party providence reaches its utter accomplishment and visibility. Industry has been pre-viewed by a scientific Intellect and constructed as a huge masterpiece. Communism claims to be a total *pro- myshlennost'* (industrialization) of life.

A campaign of mass *social engineering* took place.

A definition of the social engineering could be—power forms the people whom it represents. Party power, according to a certain ideologically justified vision, designs and materializes its own social basis. The Party imagines its constituency and proceeds with its creation. It consolidates and disciplines the historical subject summoned to fulfill the Party project. The Party has to provide itself with constituency holding the majority of the society which is automatically recruited to build up the future.

The large-scale industrialization was a political action with a single goal—to produce the Party constituency. Labor was designed to (re)produce the working-class body as the social basis of the Party. Thus Party power provided itself with historical legitimacy.

The social engineering is a creation that has a grand aesthetic element.

The reality of communism is poetically worked out. Society is a poetic work, which reproduces metaphors, not capital.

The speech figures of Party ideology are the building blocks of the mind. The key metaphors and symbols, the productive means of language, are worked out by the supreme organ of the Party politburo. It is crucial to own not the machines, but the metaphors, the means of production of symbolic meanings, not commodities. Labor forges symbols. The labor force cannot be a commodity, because it is the creator itself.

The fundamental academic field of communism lies in its political aesthetics. The political economy is a simulative one. It generates an initial appearance of an economically motivated society. Actually, it produces the symptoms of such a society, not the causes for it. The working out of metaphors and figures of speech is what generates life-forms. The identity of communism reveals itself in the overproduction of words and symbols. The political economy falsifies the genuine character of communism.

The idea became quite widespread that we are living in an actually fulfilled utopia. The common idea, that communism was impending, prevented us from seeing that we were actually in it. All the key metaphors of communist utopia have turned into reality, something which will be discussed further on. We made it through fraternity, equality, the liquidation of money, the disappearance of the state, of property, of economic structures. We experienced the conjuring trick of communism. We attempted to build it and to live in it. We survived in it.

Utopia is both poetic and political genre. It is just that, a genre which has its own structure and generates its own metaphors. Utopia compensates for the displeasure of the superimposed power structure by inventing a fictional perspective of life: an impossible perspective, which helps us to bear the actual order of life and to criticize it from the standpoint of another, unreal but cherished order of life. The transformation of utopian structures into genuinely political structures creates a society based on political aesthetic and political rhetorical principles not on economic ones. In such a society, power immediately reigns over bodies with words. It reigns over the social processes through the conjuring of language. It spellbinds.

The final objective that justifies this reality is not the legal order, but the mummy of the Leader. The mummy objectivizes political power. It is the superior body. The Party power finds its radical representation in the mummy. The political aesthetics of society reaches its sublime terms in the spectacle of the mummified Leader.

Political economy deals with idealized economic models, political aesthetics with corporeality made eternal. Political aesthetics deals with mummified bodies, objects, spaces which eternalize the strong presence of communism on earth.

At home, everyone has a measure, which he or she uses to ascertain the real dimensions in space. But somewhere out there, kept in special conditions is the ideal measure. Its length is a convention. It is the original only by virtue of a social agreement.

Everyone has at home images and words of Lenin. They are signs, allegorical instruments, which testify to the existence of the original. The original Lenin is kept in a mausoleum and is a unique, not a conventional body. A mummified uniqueness spellbinds the space embracing it. His images and his words, spread everywhere, is the radiation which imbues minds with communism.

The reality of the communist experiment is guaranteed by the magic reality of the body, stuck to the magic words of the primordial experimenter. Lenin is the author of communism. His immortalized body perpetually authorizes and legitimizes the Party. That is why the mummy must immediately be appropriated and registered in the Party inventory.

The problem of the political aesthetics of society is far more general than the problem of communism. In a historical perspective, the merging of the political and aesthetic projects for creation of a purely novel society-poem has existed as a process even before its actual accomplishment in 1917 in Russia. One of the characteristics of modernist culture at the beginning of this century was the idea of radical liquidation of the inherited structures and the generation of a bold phantasm for the organizing of an unprecedented society.

This radical phantasm creates is own genre: the manifesto. The manifesto is the verbal radicalization of the modernist vision and immediately builds the political aesthetics of the modernist endeavor. With a closer look into the different political and aesthetic manifestos, we could reconstruct a global modernist project for an unprecedented corporal integrity of society and for the daring act of building it.

In respect to this global project, political Dadaism in Berlin and the Proletcult in Russia during the 20s have quite decisive roles. The programs and projects of these two movements present to us a decisive merger of political and aesthetic ideas, of the concepts of artistic and civil action. The perfect manifestation of such a merging can be seen in the manifesto of the Berlin Dadaists Hausmann and Huelsenbeck— *"What is Dadaism and what does it want in Germany."*

A special exhibition of "degenerate," that is, modernist art mounted by the Nazis in 1937, featured other modernists on the Dada wall— painters who had nothing to do with Dadaism. This was not accidental, for Dada was exposed on the wall as the greatest disgrace most severely condemned by the Nazis.

Dada is a condenser of the modernist project. It radicalized the programs of other trends and assembled them within a political machine. It was short-lived (about six years, from 1916 to 1922) and made possible the major trends in the visual arts of late capitalism: pop art, performance, happening, assemblage, photo montage, clip, and so on. Dada radically changed the life/art relation, and transformed the figure of the artist into a brutal activist attached to (not detached from) life as a preposterous punk.

Dada is a re-active phenomenon in character. In this sense, it lacks the phenomenology of the classical type of trends. It is wrong to treat Dada as a crazy isolated phenomenon, a curio from an eccentric culture. This is precisely why this study will try to discuss Dada's cultural manifestation as maximizing the modernist projects, its principles, expressive devices and directions for political and aesthetic action. Dada is not just an artistic trend as it is usually presented on the basis of its Parisian version.

The 1920s saw the birth of a powerful political art both in Russia and Germany, an art which deliberately scrapped the border between artistic and political action. This political art was subsequently repressed by "Party" art. Nazi and Bolshevik partisanship in the arts, imposed through administrative channels by Hitler in Germany and by Stalin in Russia, liquidated political art.

It is symptomatic that Nazi Germany repressed political Dadaism, whilst the same happened to the Proletcult in Russia, liquidated by Lenin. Party policy abolished political art, especially proletarian art. This will be discussed in more detail later. For the moment I will say only that identifying the principles of political art with the principles of Party art is a gross error. Of course, the Nazis as well as Bolsheviks turned into reality many of the radical metaphors and visions of modernism, of futurism, of constructivism, of political Dadaism. The political aesthetics of communism manifests the most terrorist recurrence of the modernist phantasms.

My point is that the principles of Party art cancel the principles of modernist art, that is, that art in which visions and metaphors of future radical change arise. In short, totalitarianism as a kind of realization of the political aesthetics of modernism arrested modernist art.

In this respect, Lenin is an interesting case. He is the man whom the Dadaists in Zurich pointed out as the greatest Dada on earth. Political Dadaism in Berlin embraced the ideas of Lenin and gradually melted into the radical communist movement. Lenin was directly involved in the proletarian modernization of the political ideas of that time. That same Lenin carried out the Bolshevization (read modernization) of life through a radical act: the Revolution. After performing it that same Lenin devised Party policy as the rule of the starving Bolshevik lands. Party policy liquidated the processes of modernization.

Lenin's mummy blocks any further modernization. In it, the political and the aesthetic merge as the ultimate Party body. The mummy of Lenin is the point at which modernization is terminated and the omnipresence of the Party is imposed. This is the very point at which the idea of a political modernization of society terminates in a totalitarian mummified communism.

Communism realized a radical aesthetic, noneconomic modernization of society.

# 1

# Revolutionary Merger
of the Political and the Aesthetic

Dada emerges as an international movement in Zurich in 1916, in reaction to the World War and as a reactive concerted action of radical leftist and anarchist intellectuals of different nationalities and styles who were in Zurich at that time.

Dada is a reaction against bourgeois culture. Dada modernizes the world in an insolent antibourgeois style. The motives of artistic action are far wider than the territory of art. Dada presents itself as a daring intervention which will cure humanity of bourgeois dementia, such as politics, art, morality. Dada will chase away the monsters which have crawled out on the earth's surface, such as imperialism, Victorian morals and prejudices, together with the chef d'oeuvres of classical art. Dada acts; it doesn't produce works of art. Dada shakes up the stiff corpse of European culture. It tramples on sanctimonious bourgeois morality. It seethes in the cells of the healthy bourgeois brain. Dada blocks the logical train of thought and thus frees the human being from its importunate training in common sense.

Dada stripped tabooed organs, objects and actions naked, introducing a new material in art which was base and depressing by bourgeois moral standards. Through its blatant musculature of expression, Dada carried to the extreme limit the unrestrained collective will to mock the bourgeois individual cocooned in his morality.

Tristan Tzara arrived in Paris from Zurich. Tzara is seen as a leading Dadaist which he was—but he was an exponent of a certain French version of Dadaism. Parisian Dadaists, including Tzara's main rival, André Breton, concentrated on the techniques of insolent preposterous humor and nonsense under the direct influence of Breton's friend Jacques Vachais. The Paris-based magazine *Litterature* attracted a group subscribing to shock humor and bizarre actions. Influenced by psychoanalysis and Bergson, this group evolved the technique of *automatic writing* and free association. Dadaists turned themselves into devices and automata registering their own impulses, into wires transmitting the will to life through their resistance. That is precisely why Dadaists did not create works of art by laws inherent to art itself but, so to speak, brazenly accumulated interesting documentation on their brutal genius. Dada is a campaign which leaves an archive rather than museum exhibits and works of art.

Unlike all other Dadaist groups and centers, the Berlin wing was very active politically and charged with ultra-Bolshevism. Events in Russia ultimately politicized the programs of Berlin Dadaists. During the revolution in Germany, Huelsenbeck was proclaimed Commissar of the Arts. Hausmann adopted the pseudonym of "Dadasov." Later a large part of the Berlin wing got direct political assignments from the communist movement.

The demand for political efficiency in artistic action leads Dadaist techniques to decisive public operations and offensives which undermine the bourgeois political system, the bourgeois moral imperative and the phantoms of bourgeois art. All of this helps adapt the project to the radical modernization of society. The will that modernizes society is syncretic in its nature. In it, the aesthetic and the political are inseparable. The chief materialization of this will are photo montage, propaganda posters, allegorical constructions and assemblages of machinery which disturb the bourgeois order of things. Industry, art and politics are three heads of a single body, in the throes of one and the same will to modernization.

An exhibition of Soviet avant-garde art was held in Berlin in 1922. Arriving with the exhibition, constructivist Lisitskii started publishing, along with Yerenburg, the magazine *Veshch'* (Object) which introduced the West to modern art in Soviet Russia. The spirit of constructivism, new objectivity and new materiality promoted by *Veshch'* was already popular among Berlin Dadaists. Russian constructivist Tatlin was a dominant influence on the first Dada fair in Berlin in 1920.

Political Dadaism is infected by the ideas of machinism and the organizational theories of the Russian constructivists, obviously mixed with the organizational theories of the Proletcult and its ideologist Bogdanov. Constructivist art neither embellishes life, nor creates works beyond it. It organizes life completely. In its aesthetics, the geometrical and the political mind coincide. Constructivism is a syncretic state of science and politics. The modernization of society is guaranteed by such mergers of science, art and politics.

If constructivism is called the socialism of vision, then Dadaism could be called the Bolshevism of action. In Germany Dada is taken over by Bolshevik visions of a "laboroid" space assembled of flesh and metal, of bodies and aggregates, of scaffolds and machines, of clenched fists and chanting mouths. In Berlin, Dada organizes political attractions, mounts centaurs of bodies and machines, in order to make a show of the magic of the endless proletarian feats of labor.

Constructivism and Dadaism, those kindred trends, formally met in Weimar in 1922.

George Grosz published his collection *The Face of the Ruling Class*, which Lenin enjoyed immensely, in 1922 and 1923. A year after, he became the leader of the Red Group of artists ancillary to the German Communist Party.

If Parisian Dada died with the advent of surrealism, in Germany it acted as a combination of political constructivism, proletarianization of the visual and objective world and industrialization of the artistic performance.

Dadaists Hausmann, Hannah Hoech, Hans Richter and Kurt Schwitters later formed the core of German constructivism. In Berlin, meanwhile, expressionism was just as powerful, its left wing being definitely political and far from alien to the idea of a mass political feat of the proletariat. However, Dada attacked expressionism. This is entirely understandable considering Dada's sympathies for constructivism. Dada attacked expressionism precisely through constructivism. It attacked expressionism for its exalted phony imagery that expresses a sick inside, for rejecting the factual zone of life and the objects which populate it. Machinism and rationalism, the mainstays of constructivist organizational theory, were naturally hostile towards euphoric expressions and visions.

Art works directly on the factual plane of life, and the sights it leaves there and the visions it evokes should not stun. They should canvass. They activate the work of reason rather than the morbid imagination. Reason is the supreme motor of the creating human body. The first International Dada Fair featured a poster which read *"Art is dead. Long live Tatlin's new machine art."* Exhibits at this fair included impressive collages, photo montages, photo attractions of participants themselves; their bodies; workaday, everyday objects and contraptions; propaganda posters and dummies; installations and aggregates which could be operated, destroyed or at least touched; the blasphemies of the Dadaists themselves. The factuality of life was turned into a circus, into circus tricks, attractions, an orgy of objects. This was the political circus of life.

Contrary to leftist political expressionism, Dada is remarkably resilient. After the tramping of the revolutionary movement in Germany, some of the expressionists retire, others commit suicide, still others sink into a deep mysticism. Dada, on the contrary, experiences exasperation. It accuses expressionism of consecration of the sick inside of man, of whimpering over its Gothic structures. Dada has no illusions. Dada does not suffer from any prophetic spirit. Dada is a saboteur and is oriented externally, towards expansion. During these years of social shock, the ontology of the world changes for the expressionists—which destroys them. For Dada, the only thing that changes is the direction of the proletarian strike, and that doesn't in the least make them turn off the engines. Because the noise of the engines manifests the (idio)syncrasis of the political, industrial and aesthetic modernization of the world.

The athletic proletarian body molds details from metal and with a geometrical precision puts together machines with which to attack the complacency of the senile world. Dada amplifies to the extreme ideology and practice of the creator—the machinist.

*Since machinery is the soul of the modern world, and*
*since the genius of machinery attains its highest expres-*
*sion in America, why is it not reasonable to believe*
*that in America the art of the future will flower most*
*brilliantly?*

*F. Picabia (in Kuenzli 1986)*

Dada spread fast in New York thanks to the arrival of European Dadaists like Marcel Duchamp, Man Ray, Francis Picabia and Arthur Craven. That this Dadaist wing was leftist radical is evident by Man Ray's recollections of the Dadaist newspaper which he used to publish: "The heading consisted of three black letters: TNT. It was a political paper with a very radical slant. The words Communism and Bolshevism didn't exist then in America. TNT was a tirade against industrialists, the exploiters of workers. We were all mixed up with the anarchist group. It was anarchism rather than anything else." (in Kuenzli 1986, 146).

In New York—this stunning artifact of the industrial machine age, this mammoth realization of constructivist reason and ultimate crowding of bodies, objects and apparatuses—Dadaists found their ultimate project fulfilled. Duchamp saw his "ready-mades" on a giant scale, the mass production of identical artifacts, streams of ready-to-wear and modular space assemblages. All in all, geometrical reason has tailored titanic spaces and artifacts, buildings and prospects through its ingenious prostheses: machines, automata, cranes. Picabia saw his machine visions operating on a mass scale. The new materiality, new objectivity and new media unfolds the city's unprecedented space. New York is a unique fold—not in the earth's crust, but in the industrial massif of civilization. All suggestions for a natural essence of spatial rhythm are dispelled. The motors of this awesome swelling relief are industry and politics. They are the motors which Dada forces to the brink of a radical accident.

Political scandal, abolishing natural geometry, uprising of the objective order: all these actions Dada deployed on the relief of civilization.

# The Political Aesthetics of Modernization

## THE MAGIC OF THE APPARATUSES

*The establishing of a class bond that is visual (kino-eye)
and auditory (radio-ear) between the proletarians of all
nations and all lands, based on the platform of the communist decoding of the world—this is our objective.*
*Dziga Vertov (1984, 50)*

Dada appears in an age already proclaimed futuristic. It extols the
beauty of war; mass man's athleticism; synthetic materials; mechanized voice—radio and megaphones; the machine eye—photo
and movie cameras. The legacy of modernism has also been ab-
sorbed incorporated in the political programs of parties and organizations to set the world straight and replace it with a radically
new world, a Brave New World. Marinetti extols war as a natural
excess of the senses, of the machinism and communal athleticism
of bodies. War is the remarkable transgression through which politics is wholly transformed into aesthetics, and political passion into
immediately aesthetic passion. Political interest contorts in a sublime military convulsion and spews forth the charred images of the
new world.

## THE MACHINE

*We cannot improve the making of our eye, but we can
endlessly perfect the camera. The weakness of the human eye is manifest. We affirm the kino-eye.*
*Dziga Vertov (1984, 15–16)*

In it the human is overcome. The organic is surpassed by the mechanical. In the machine, life reaches its ultimate organization. The human
body is merely an organ of the machine. The organic element is one of
the nodes of a mechanic totality. Only now and now at last is the mind
freed from the pathetic body and moves into a dwelling organized and
invented by itself—the machine.

The Machinist is superman. The Machinist is not subject to subconscious repression or guilt; he is not infected by individuality or sensi-
tivity. The Machinist is the creator of the modernized age; he has
decisively overthrown the yoke of the sniffling sentimentality of his
perverse body, its ugly organs bandaged with the outfits of culture—

clothing. The Creator Machinist represents the mass superorganization of bodies. In this sense, he himself is not a separate body. He is the radically organized state of the laboring bodies with a machinelike principle of common action.

The creative body attains a communal machinelike physiognomy never seen before. In it, the political and the aesthetic are one.

### OCULUS EX MACHINA

*I am a mechanical eye.*
*I, a machine, show you the world*
*as only I can see it.*
          *Dziga Vertov (1984, 17)*

Eyeglasses are a prosthesis to the eye. They help it see. The still and movie cameras are the superprostheses of the eye. Through them, the eye overcomes its human principle of seeing and becomes a machine. The eye itself becomes Machinist. In this sense, it becomes collective, because it overcomes its individual being, its pathetic partiality and lachrymality. The eye begins to see objectively.

The camera's objective lens overcomes the eye's organic optics. The objective lens is a crystal absolute. It is a superindividual organization of sight. It is the unified being of all possible eyes. The object-glass is the new communal constructivism of sight. It is the ultimately modernized liturgical eye. The Cyclops.

The camera is a prosthesis which has reached its perfection. Its superhuman ingenuity has radically supplanted the function of the organ. The principle of this self-activating prosthesis manifests the essence of the new agent of modernization. The new communal medium. The mass medium.

The "objective genius" manifests in itself the political order of things. It is the assembly line of interlinking *attractions*. Eisenstein's "montage of attractions" ingeniously accomplished in *Potemkin*, for example, is a manifestation of the contemporary political flux.

According to the classical bourgeois intuition "the subjective genius of art" cannot be political, in that it opens and guards the eternal, age-old order of things. In principle, it transcends the political and the eye opens itself to eternity. "Subjective genius" does not rest on montages and collages, on cutting out and pasting up shocking pictures, on attractions. It rests on the internal integrity of the chef d'oeuvres. It could not stand prostheses.

Inversely, the political art represents an ultimately focused objective genius, driven by the performance of wonderful aggregates, contraptions and linkages, by the vision of unseen laboring automata which modernize the procession of life. In general, the idea of world modernization is of inordinate political relevance.

The eye becomes agent of the objective lens. The organ appropriates the principle of action of the prosthesis. The natural is overcome. Objective vision marks a decisive victory of the unified automatic mass principle, that stems not from the integrity of bourgeois genius, but from the rhythmic action of the apparatuses.

Objectivity originates in the Machine, which has radically overthrown the Human. Thus, the objective world is always produced and never found. The modernization of the world is represented as mass production of objectivity.

Political Dada does not make mere collages of things and baubles. The world in which Dada raves is not the mercantile world of things; it is not the space of the bourgeois and of things drawn into a small private world. The world is industrial, labor communal, objective; things are uniform, not unique. They reflect mass industrial relations. This is a world in which uniformity reigns. Dada attacks the production of linear uniformity. It attacks common standards of vision. It takes over the objective eye, takes over the forms of mass consciousness. It accomplishes a wild pastiche of details and documents, of pieces and industrial refuse. This is a circus of industrially produced uniformity, a sudden breakdown of the prostheses which stimulates an erotic shuddering in the organs supported by them.

The camera's objective lens forms a link between the eye and the view. The change in the optics of the objective lens makes the link move. The objective lens is an Eye-Centaur who gallops.

The view, as well as the eye, is an agent of the optic structure of the objective lens. Political Dadaism does not merely probe your eyes or break objects. It attacks the objective structure of vision—the conjuncture formed by the eye and the object in the photograph. It attacks the photograph, that is, the linking of eye with view. Dada is a decisive intervention in the link. It dismantles it by a kick.

Photo montages, splicing and gluing, the retailoring of ready-made reality—this is the new artistic technique. Objectively snapped reality can only be recut, it cannot be recreated. The reality, which appears through the action of the machine reactivates the action of the scissors and the saw, not of the brush and carver. Cutting and fracturing, bandaging and plastering, affixing prostheses—this is the political orthopedics of modernism.

## THE CUTS OF THE COLLAGE

*He spoke about a surgical intervention in the grand or-
ganism of literature and life, and to prove his operation
just [Pravda] he cited by heart a series of excerpts from
the works of world-famous surgeons.*

*V. Kamenskii (1940, 59)*

The eye, armed with scissors and saw, insolently trespasses the spaces
of objective reality by fracturing objects, and then proceeds with plasters, bandages and prostheses. The scissors, this tireless guillotine, is the
magical instrument of modernization. The diaphragm of the photo
camera is an eye turned into scissors. It cuts off, like a guillotine, pieces
of the vision—frames, snapshots. The diaphragm performs a spasm and
contracts the vision. This contracted and cut-off view must be bandaged
and fortified with prostheses. Then comes the magic of pastiche, which
reassembles the view chopped up in the camera.

The vision of the artist cannot be embodied in a picture. It can be re-
joined after it has been fractured and dismembered by the diaphragm.
In this political surgery of sight, the view acquires a distorted body.
From this comes the feeling of a disparate and then indecently cobbled
together defective vision of the artist in political art. It is this principle
of vision which Nazism attacks later from its party position, in order to
liquidate the political art of modernism.

## THE NEW AUTHENTICITY: JUSTICE OF SCISSORS

*the FACTORY OF FACTS.*

*Filming facts. Sorting facts. Disseminating facts. Agi-
tating with facts. Propaganda with facts. Fists made
of facts.*

*Dziga Vertov (1984, 59)*

The modern age establishes a brand new notion of "fact," "objectivity,"
"authenticity," "documentation" and "technical reproduction of facts."
The transmission of information becomes a problem of the media, not
of personae. The principles of reporting and documenting events is
completely mechanized: machine voices, microphones, sequential
views, wave transmission. The collage principle of broadcasting reports
induces the impression of their autonomy and causal independence.
They coexist, concur and associate in the flux of information disregard-
ing any speculative holistic picture of the world.

The classical intuition of the organic integrity of the world is abolished by the vision of the objective-collage structure of the world and its political design as the motor of progress. The intuitions of sacral continuity and immanent providence are replaced by visions of collage discreteness and political plannings. Authenticity is supplanted by the media.

"They" see design rather than providence, facts rather than truth, objects rather than organs of the infinite world body.

The mammoth archive of the world swells every minute: facts, evidence, reports. What testifies and verifies the actual picture of the world is its File. We dwell in it: a File-World with perfectly developed media of tracking, deletion, documentation, registration, cataloguing.

### THE NEWSPAPER

The newspaper is doubtless a collage of documents and reports, interpretations and news, type and photos. It does not represent and manifest the sacral continuity and causality of events in the world.

The paper documents facts and presents interpretations. The interpretation of a fact does not substitute the fact itself—it adjoins within a collage, stuck on it like an outfit. The collage structure generates a new intuition of authenticity—the truth (*Pravda*) of scissors and gluing.

The world is not divinely providential per se. It is a dynamic constellation of a multitude of ad hoc political designs and interests. The newspaper is a predetermined space. The exact location of a fact or document determines its political implication. Thus the paper designs the political appearance of the today's world. The papers are shots in a reel with meaningful assemblage. The newspaper is a political "attraction" inducing ideological conclusions.

*Attraction . . . is every aggressive moment . . . which*
*acts upon the spectator's senses or psychology, an effect*
*which is experimentally verified and mathematically*
*calculated with a view to causing definite emotional*
*shocks to the perceiver; which makes possible the percep-*
*tion of the ideas of the things demonstrated—the final*
*ideological conclusion.*
*Sergei Eisenstein, 1923 (1964, 269–73)*

However, let us harbor no illusion that this political aesthetics of newspapers lasts long. In totalitarian societies where the idea of "Party" *Pravda* (truth) abolishes all others, the newspaper formally preserves its collage appearance. Party Truth and Justice (*Pravda*) justifies the Party design for permanent usurpation of power, control over all spheres of life, inaugurating mandatory ideological figures, metaphors, images and interpretations. The totalitarian newspaper does not proceed from the political flux of facts and documents. Facts serve the implicit or explicit Party design. The Party-minded newspaper is a monumental work for it represents the Party mold of the world.

The communist papers publicize the one Party interest. Those papers do not report facts but rather their mandatory interpretations. They do not document events but their Party significance. Facts or documents cannot be credible in these papers. Only their interpretation is either credible or not. The totalitarian newspaper does not misinform. It performs the Party function. Communism is not politically discrete, but homogeneous for it expresses the unified Party will to power. Every day the newspaper informs the population about a single fact: the Party is in power.

## THE CLASSICAL/MODERNIZED WORK

*Crystallize man not by a single "synthetic" portrait,*
*but by a whole lot of snapshots taken at different times*
*and in different conditions.*
                    A. Rodchenko (Bowlt 1988, 254)

The lofty classical notion of a work of art, of a creation, enacts an inherently complete and self-sufficient entity with its own order—beginning, progression, end and self-enclosing space. The creation is perfect in its finality, proportion and integrity.

Contrary to the act of creation, everyday life is dissipation. The constitution of the artistic entity has nothing to do with the constitution of facts in life. Creation manifests the principle of being. Thus creation testifies per se to the veritable order of the world. It is itself a travesty of the *logos.* The creation conjures up an otherwise boundless entity making it commensurate with the small-sized human being. In this sense the creation is not grounded in the everyday course of life. Everyday life strands us amid singularities and partialities. The creation builds universal forms. We face what is made invisible and unrecognizable in the course of profane life.

The classical notion of a creation is based on the radical discrimination between facts of life and facts of art. These two realms of being are regulated by different orders and rules. The modern age has started demolishing this border.

This study will not dwell on the history of the issue. The important point is that Dada brought the "world of creation" to catastrophe because it is precisely this world that decrees art as a superdisciplined and superordered activity. The creative work is a barracks. Poetics is a command. Creativity is disciplined by a multitude of orders, rules and laws. Not for Dada. As far as Dada is concerned, the artistic act does not happen beyond the course of life. It is the maximum of life.

The artistic is closely related to the erotic: *eroticism* unbandages the cultural plasters of these body parts treated by the public as bruises, wounds and fractures of morals.


## PHOTO


*And show me where, and when, and of which artistically synthetic work one could say: this is the real V.I. Lenin.*

*There is not one. And there will not be—because there is a file of photographs, and this file of snapshots allows no one to idealize or falsify Lenin. . . . no one would allow artistic nonsense to be taken for the eternal Lenin.*

*A. Rodchenko (Bowlt 1988, 254)*

The magic of the photographic plate imposes an inverted notion of "an original" in art. Unlike the classical creation as an immediate manifestation of essence, the photo is a substitution of life authenticity by a picture directly derived from profane reality. The photo is a shot phantom from the world of appearance. The photo is a void original for it bears the appearance of something which has vanished. It could be an original only by force of a convention, not by its material.

The virtual original retains a physical uniqueness. In this respect the negative is the photographic original. From an aesthetic perspective, however, the negative is an absolutely "reversed" excerpt from the entire picture of life. This excerpt becomes aesthetically representative only when developed. Various positive prints are something like phantoms of the original negative that could change and be different. In this respect the photographic original is shaken to the utmost insofar as it is in force only when subsequently developed and released through phantoms. The magic of the photographic plate stems from its *negative aesthetic representation*. It is a negative vision of life.

In brief, the photographic original is nothing but a mold that manufactures pictures and is significant as a technological curio. In contrast, the classical original is not an off-print of any event or a generator of phantom copies. It conveys being, not appearance in life.

Another peculiarity of classical art is that the borders of the work do not encompass in time and place the act of creation itself. The

chrono-topos of creation lays beyond the boundaries of the work insofar as the creator is located in life with his/her body and beyond it with
his/her genius. The modernist creation, in contrast, gets the creator's
body involved. This is precisely why the creation is an action, not an artifact beyond life. The creator is nowhere else but here, in the work, neither before nor behind it. This is the principle of the performance,
happening, action. The first Dada fair was precisely such an action.
Those actions do not have meanings; they have political design. They
canvass and instigate.

### THE EROTIC REVOLT OF THE OBJECTS

*The shadow cast by a four-dimensional figure on our
space is a three-dimensional shadow. . . .
     The set of these three-dimensional perceptions of
the four-dimensional figure would be the foundation for
a reconstruction of the four-dimensional figure.*
                    *Marcel Duchamp (Kuenzli 1986, 55)*

The eye recognizes only the three-dimensional shadows of four-dimensional figures. The eye actually sees negatives. The question is how the
eye can unfold the fourth dimension out of what it sees or how to develop this vision. The three-dimensional objects that swim into view are
allegorical figures open to their four-dimensional completeness. The
eye must try to extrapolate the fourth dimension.

Marcel Duchamp is best known for his ready-mades: mass-produced artifacts which congest the space and create mass automatic
habits of eyes and bodies of those who use them. The trick of the mass
product is that it is no longer noticed precisely because of its regular
everyday automatic usage. The body stops feeling its own prostheses
which guide and control its actions. These mass-produced series of
identical forms occupy the vision. The eye coasts along a vast objective
field without even noticing it. We can say that this is the trick of the
three-dimensional constitution of space: to discipline an automatic vision and automatic body habit on a mass scale. The three-dimensional
space is stuffed with mass-produced and mass-used ready-mades.

In order to develop the fourth dimension, the eye and the body
must be prevented from using the objects correctly. Three-dimensional
space is regulated by the correct automatic usage of the objects. The
fourth dimension emerges when the automaton fails since precisely this
failure opens the eye to four-dimensional space. The new modern age
does not need new objects, even though they be objects d'art. The world
has been stuffed and turned into a storehouse. Art must de-automatize

the objects already there and the visions and bodies related to them. In this sense, art is an action on, rather than a production of objects. It triggers catastrophes of automata by the shock of the vision penetrating the four-dimensional space.

The emergence of the fourth dimension is caused by the breakdown of the automatic usage of the objects. Duchamp—he takes an urinal and entitles it *Fountain.* This urinal is a ready-made installed in the public lavatories of mass industrial urban space. Duchamp confronts the eye with this urinal in a public place where the body cannot do what it has always done in the "other" place. The reflex of excretion is prompt but so is the prohibition of its gratification. The breakdown emerges because of the conflict between the impulse of the eye and that of the excretory system. The title, *Fountain,* causes another shock. The name has not been merely replaced. The urinal is labeled with a name which assigns it right the opposite action: not a funnel which drains the discharge but which spews it. Reading the title, the eye is panic-stricken, exposed to the danger of being splashed. This geyser-urinal is an allegory of the revolt of objects. The fourth dimension might prove the presence of a will in the object which we have never ascribed to it.

Let us examine another of Duchamp's masterpieces— *Large Glass* or its full title: *The Bride Stripped Bare by Her Bachelors, Even.* It is even, big, transparent, flat glass. A bizarre machine-like figure is engraved on it. We assume that the glass is a two-dimensional space on which a three-dimensional figure casts its shadow. The figure in the flat transparent glass is such a shadow or a *negative* through which the eye must extrapolate the missing dimension of the object thus developing its *positive.* The large glass must be developed. Duchamp loved having photos (shadows) of ready-mades at home. *Large Glass* is precisely such a photo (shadow).

*Large Glass* is also a showcase but a special one. Nothing is displayed behind it. What is behind is invisible. This showcase projects just the silhouettes of the objects displayed behind it. The exhibits are displayed as allegorical figures engraved on the showcase itself.

The figure depicted in *Large Glass* is no doubt an erotic one: this is a "sex machine." The bride stripped bare by her bachelors is presented as a puppet machine. The various units and joints of this machine are ready-made objects bound and activated through transmissions. This is an allegorical orgy of objects which the eye must recognize as fornication. A "sex machine" which must be recognized as an organic act.

The machine is an allegorical showcase of the organic; the ready-made object—of the human body—and the transmission—of copulation. The erection of the fourth-dimensional body is erotic.

The world is transparent. What is not transparent are the shadows of "something" invisible in this world. "Something" which is lost in the world transparency. Thus every visible object is an allegory which figures the invisible and prompts the eye to plunge into it.

## REVOLUTIONARY DEVICES

### THE DEVICE AS A STRATAGEM

*The purpose of art is to make us see, not recognize,*
*things; the device proper of art is the de-familiarization*
*of things and the encumbered form which makes percep-*
*tion a harder and longer process.*
    *Art is a way to experience the making of things,*
*what is already made in art is of no importance.*
        *V. Shklovskii, "Art as Device" (1980, 334–42)*

In 1919 Shklovskii published a small essay titled "Art as Device." It is considered to be the major manifesto of the formal school which aspires to shake up the senile and sclerotic field of art criticism. In it he claims that art criticism has lost its proper object and urgently needs to regain it, to recognize it anew. The problems of art criticism stem from the fact that it, in a historically developed self-oblivion, has neglected the art itself and substituted issues borrowed from secondary fields—such as psychology, sociology and cultural studies.

The first thing to be done is to abstract *differentia specifica* of art which could demarcate it from the zone of everyday life. Art makes a great difference precisely against the background of everyday life.

Let us summarize the basic discrepancy between everyday life and art: Life presents facts that are self-evident the way they appear. Art devises conjuring tricks, stunning skills and worlds never seen before. Life implies automatic recognition of the realities. Art implies contemplation, vision, abstention from utilizing them. Art blocks any automatic recognition and consumption of its pieces. Life communicates perception with familiar phenomena. Art de-familiarizes and excommunicates its objects by giving them estranged shapes and never tested properties. Life is an automated zone where everything works as if by itself and in accordance with an unfathomable principle. Art makes things work in an unpredictable and unprecedented manner, making no accordance with any general or particular law of life.

Man slides over the sur-face of everyday realities using different facilities that diminish friction. Inversely, man encounters the rugged face of art where friction and resistance are utterly maximized. Life is a prefigured phenomenon. Art is a puzzle. Life facilitates existence. Art perplexes it. In life the principle of the minimum resistance rules, in art—the maximum resistance of the material.

*Device* is termed the constitutional unit of art. It is an invention designed on purpose to block out the principle of everyday life. The artist creates a whole set of artful plots and artifices in order to discriminate art from everyday life. Device is the *differentia specifica* of art and art criticism must become aware of it.

The artist, as opposed to the agent of everyday life, breaks into its automation using special techniques, stunning gear and equipment. According to this creative strategy, art is a *techne* and the artist is a *master* of an action that breaks through the thick flow of everyday life and brings turbulence into it. Art as *techne* fits together arbitrary devices that take over the causal principle of everyday life. The artist as master conducts the emergence and the expansion of this planned arbitrariness. Hence, revolution could be considered as a performance with the same features and effects as art.

The device does not trigger but rather targets the automation of life. It encumbers life imposing maximal retardation or deceleration, deviation and suspension of its strictly directed and channeled flow. We recover from life through art. We need to retrieve our initial ability to see and to wonder, not to recognize and to label things using ready-made patterns. The encumbered recognition stimulates vision. The suspended recognition urges device making. The device resembles a miraculous prosthesis assembled in the organism of life that makes life act in a stunning way or blocks its functions and generates a sudden unprecedented performance. This makes you see things bare without being forced to recognize them. According to Shklovskii the ultimate goal of art is a device to be invented and not an image to be drawn. The device generates *vision* and not *recognition* of things (*veshchi kak videnie, a ne kak uznavanie*).

The artful *device* triggers vision through estrangement and defamiliarization of things but not recognition through their probable appearance. The device inaugurates absolute discrepancy and repudiates everyday common sense decorum and rationality. The device could be termed *organon* not in the sense of an organ that belongs to an organic entity but in its other meaning of a "battle machine" that destroys walls and breaks into the fortifications of the stronghold called everyday life. More than this, the master exposes the devices that have been invented and worked out, lays them bare and thus stimulates thought. All that props up a work, all what justifies the composition of devices, all what motivates the plot—the whole is laid demonstratively bare so that the spectator can contemplate the very formation of art, the very composition of the work as a thing different in its origin and goal orientation from what life is.

The doctrine for art formation is the doctrine for life transformation.

## DEVICE AND V-EFFECT

*Zeigt das Zeigen! Show that you are showing! You
should not forget the attitude of showing. The attitude
of showing should be basic to all other attitudes.*
                    Brecht (Wulbern 1971, 71)

A similar idea occurred to B. Brecht. He formulated the famous *V-effect (Verfremdungseffekte)* as opposed to the Aristotelian mimesis and "dramatic" effect of art. Julian Wulbern in his book *Brecht and Ionesco* sums it up—"Verfremdung, intentional destruction of the illusion of reality or of dramatic continuity, though of course for strictly ironic effect" (p. 64). "Perversion of logic, destruction of familiar relationships, and distortion of the traditional patterns of language" (p. 66).

V-effect targets to expose through de familiarization of the automatic principle and hidden motor of everyday life realities, to estrange the implied politics in everything that happens. V-effect makes the machine of life visible, makes you realize its principle and makes you plan how to improve, how to repair or, eventually, how to replace it. The anti-Aristotelian idea for a mimesis that terrifies not the senses but the intellect of the spectators Brecht has elaborated in his article *"The Street Scene: A Basic Model for an Epic Theater"* (1968, 85–96). Mimesis is understood as a political act of estrangement from the everyday flux of life that exposes its automation. This is the conceptual core of the essay:

> The actor used a somewhat complex technique to detach himself from the character portrayed . . . 'see things a different way'
>
> It is most important that one of the main features of the ordinary theater should be excluded from our street scene: the engineering of illusion. The street demonstrator's performance is essentially repetitive. The event has taken place; what you are seeing now is a repeat.
>
> We now come to one of those elements that are peculiar to the epic theater, the so-called V-effect (Verfremdung). What is involved here is, briefly, a technique of taking the human social incidents to be portrayed and labeled as something striking, something that calls for explanation, is not to be taken for granted, not just natural.

There is one thing more that we need to make the picture of the epic theater complete—the concept termed *gestus.* Brecht in his outspoken *Little Organon for the Theater* coined the term: "The realm of attitudes which the characters adopt toward one another we shall call the realm of Gestus. Bodily posture, accent, and facial expression are determined by a social Gestus" (Wulbern 1971, 57).

The term *gestus* proliferates throughout his theoretical works in order to formulate a basic political understanding of life which is directly related to the V-effect of art. We could say that the epic (non-dramatic/non-Aristotelian) strategy of acting exercises an impact on the invisible dominant *gestus* which in a certain way keeps society disciplined. By means of the V-effect mimetic art exposes its hidden mechanism to the vigilant gaze of the spectator and thus makes it recognizable. Aristotelian mimesis induces terror and pity and thus purifies the soul of the spectator from the passions accumulated in the course of life. Inversely, Brecht launches a political campaign toward obscurantism through the artistic mode of mimesis. Mimesis equals de-automatization of the dominant *gestus* first through estrangement of its corporal social integrity, and then through an abstraction and manifestation of its mechanism on the stage.

Basically what we face here is a sociopolitical approach to acting. Everyday society reproduces an invisible automatic system of social habits—*gestus.* Through repetition and special techniques of de-familiarization and estrangement (V-effect), the stage makes this *gestus* demonstratively visible and exposes it to the bombarding of the critical reason. The master and the spectator have to be equally aware of what they do on both sides of the work of art—to be aware of the political assignment of art itself.

### ECONOMY OF LIFE AND ART

*Economy* was a key term that penetrated the public discourse and different works on sociology, philosophy, aesthetics, politics and so on. In Shklovskii's manifesto we find formulated two "economic principles":

1.  The economy of everyday life entails less resistance and minimum spending of life resources, sliding over the surfaces of reality and acting in accordance with the automata of the major social habits. Perpetual self-affirmation of an one-and-the-same value system and status quo.
2.  The economy of art entails utmost gratification through utter exhaustion, excessive spending, maximum resistance, strong friction between objects, languages and bodies.

Following this strategic division we could go further:

The verbal agenda of the everyday utterance is to convey maximum explicit information and contents. What matters is the specific message abstracted from any possible form of the utterance.

The verbal agenda of art is not the priority of a message, but an erotic massage of language that stimulates and propagates a hitherto unseen meaning.

One is a demonstrative and the other an informative event. One pronounces its contents and meaning. The other announces its shape. One proposes. The other exposes.

### PARODY AND IRONY IN A CLINIC OF THE ARTS

*There is a lot of talk these days about irony and humor,*
*especially by people who have never been able to practice*
*them but nevertheless know how to explain everything.*
*I am not completely unfamiliar with these two passions.*
Kierkegaard (1983, 22)

Parody and irony are special kinds of metadevices. They are devices for detecting and laying bare other devices. In an imaginary clinic of art, irony and parody would be the major methods of treatment.

Parody is a special kind of mimesis that copies devices from one work and pastes them into a different work, overexposes them by augmenting their major features, twists them, schematizes their appearance and triggers their mechanical repetition. This idea of parody was developed by Tynianov (1987, 30) who detected a figure of Dostoevskii's fiction—Foma Fomich as a parody of Gogol'.

*Parody* could repair a worn-out device by retrieving its original status of a deliberately planned unit of art. The everlasting recurrence of the device from oblivion into art goes through parody.

The realm of everyday life stores the worn-out devices abandoned by art. Using parody, art calls them back. Parody occurs when art recollects its own devices.

*Irony* in Shklovskii's understanding, opposes the naive attitude toward any specific utterance and language in general. It lays demonstratively bare the so-called motivation (justification) and the linguistic machine that manufactures any particular poetic utterances and literature in general— *Zeigt das Zeigen!*

Irony makes us abstract not *what* but *how* something has been said. It abolishes the subject matter and overexposes the speaking subject through the very formation of the utterance. Sentences mean nothing; they refer to nothing but to the speech act itself. They emerge as suggestive heraldry of the speaking subject. They testify only to the subject that utters them. The ultimate irony is a mere symptom of the condition of the speaking subject and provides no detached subject-matter.

Following Soren Kierkegaard, that theologian of irony, we could say that man is doomed to use irony in order to put indirectly what God puts directly—*Ego sum qui sum!* In man's utterance between *ego sum*—and—*qui sum* lays bare the verbal corpus of irony. Through irony the *mode* of "qui sum" is de-familiarized and alienated from the *fact* of "ego sum." The human mode of being renders Ego incognito. Ego becomes an ever-wandering stranger in the domain of being.

In *Fear and Trembling* Kierkegaard reflects on irony as an example for a radical *resignation* (alienation, estrangement, incognito) of the speaking subject from the speech act itself. Irony testifies to the fact that the speaker goes beyond language and that the act of utterance is the device by means of which he performs this. Irony provides the utterance with suggestive appearance but annihilates the immediate presence of the speaking subject himself. Irony launches the subject beyond the language and leaves the uttered matter as tokens of an inconceivable and arbitrary subjectivity. "Irony and humor are also self-reflective and thus belong to the sphere of infinite resignation; their elasticity is owing to the individual's incommensurability with actuality" (Kierkegaard 1983, 51).

Only through irony can the artist master the work. Through irony the artist overexposes the devices as the only exhibits in the space of the work. The subject-matter of the work becomes the mortal body of the eternal genius.

## ZOO LAID BARE

Shklovskii devised a work entitled *ZOO* where he reflects on irony and simultaneously performs it. Irony is equally a subject-matter of the work and a mode of the work itself. Let us dismantle the major figure in it—the title itself. Zoo has no referential meaning. It is a heraldry. It heralds the intelligence of the master that invented it. It has been drawn, not written. Let us examine the figure. It contains two circles—OO—and two angles put across each other—Z. It is an assemblage fitted together by two wheels and an angular construction.

G. Apollinaire said that the wheel was invented when man wanted to imitate walking. The wheel does not resemble the leg but was devised to imitate the motion of the leg. Mimesis performed metamorphosis not analogy, refraction not reflection—the leg was twisted into a wheel. The wheel is a prosthesis that accelerates walking and speeds up movement.

The two angles of the figure mentioned above are nothing but two crutches put together. The crutch resembles a leg much more than the wheel does. The crutch suggests a disabled leg. It makes you move much slower than by nature. The crutch signifies disability and the wheel superability of the leg. One resembles the figure of the organ, the other one transfigures it into a hitherto unseen shape that overcomes the natural principle. One is a token of the decline and the other a token of the supernatural recovery of the leg.

The device of the disabled—the two crutches—is put into a figure together with the device of the superabled—the two wheels. The figure manifests the revolution of the device.

Zoo heralds revolution.

## LEF DEVISES REVOLUTION

*It is not accidental that LEF called itself a* LEFT FRONT OF THE ARTS: *it includes in itself many different detachments—poets, artists, writers, theoreticians and so on. Each of these detachments masters a different kind of weapon—for example, among the poets we have (1) specialized laboratory workers preparing the models of the word, (2) poets of the future writing mainly about the coming day and finally (3) agitators and poster makers working on the topic of the day.*
*LEF-AGITKI (1925, 3)*

LEF—or Left Front of the Arts is an union of revolutionary artists and writers initiated in Moscow at the end of 1922 by Maiakovskii and other futurists. The idea was an universal front of the avant-garde to be established with strictly formulated strategy and goal that could put together the endeavors of various revolutionary groups from different branches of the art. The Front had to chase away the apparitions of the bourgeois vision of life. Members were such artists and writers as Pasternak, Kamenskii, Rodchenko, Stepanova, Tatlin, Brik, Shklovskii and close to this milieu were film directors like Eisenstein, Dziga Vertov, Kuleshov and Shub.

As *The Grand Soviet Encyclopedia* reports, Maiakovskii eventually realized the mistake he made and deserted.

*Condense your thoughts into a slogan.*
*Maiakovskii*

*How can we establish an audio link right along the front line of the world proletariat.*
*Dziga Vertov (1984, 56)*

The following are notes taken at the time of my journey along the trenches of the Left Front of the Arts deserted after the end of the battle. What I am aiming at is a reconstruction by using the remnants and the ruins scattered along the Front, a restoration of the battlefield by working with the objects and icons of the destruction it had caused on earth. Using the mannerism of the battle, its peculiar revolutionary *gestus*, and political jargon, using its smashed and crashed armor, let me talk about the Left Front. By not only quoting slogans but also restoring the manner of speech, let me evoke the picture of the Front, let me stage the LEF—this is the objective of the text that follows.

Keep moving along the Front from Right to Left and from the general to the particular and you will run into a dashing figure—Maiakovskii!

LEF's command:

> *to the left—*
>
> *single file—*
>
> *forward march!*
> *—LEF to Battle! (1925, 233)*

## THE TELEGRAPH: REVOLUTIONARY SPERMATIZER

*And what an outrage provoked his demand—"spermatize the poetic word."*
          *V. Kamenskii (1940, 27)*

Here I will consider the machine of the revolutionary language and its main units as something that provides the global context for the "device theory" and appoints art as a major conscious, goal oriented activity which aims at the achievement of a definite political effect. Revolution could be considered as a system of extreme devices that gradually gets normalized in a new system of society.

The flux of revolutionary time was utterly accelerated by the telegraph. It made possible the instant and exchange of information. The commands and imperatives, the messages and requests circulating through the telegraphic system were in the revolutionary language proper mastering the spontaneous flow of events. The telegraph made possible the communicability of revolutionary turbulence. It generated an unprecedented speech style characterized by an instant language. The word sent through the channels of the telegraph is supposed to be immediately performed, turned into acts. The rhetoric of the telegraph assembles such linguistic devices which are to invade the flux of the

Revolution in order to channel its direction or to conduct it toward a strategic end. This word is charged with an enormous Will to be performed and materialized right away, to be turned into action at once and thus to overtake the spontaneous turmoil. This word drives the Revolution.

The revolutionary speedy word penetrated the whole body of letters and agitated a drastic political acceleration of life. The outpouring of slogans, advertisements, leaflets, and handouts resembles a perpetually gushing ejaculation caused by the machine (the telegraph) that disseminates genes of revolution all over the world.

This word is to be ultimately short, broadcasting maximum information, imposing maximum will, having maximum strategic meaning and purpose. The telegraph is the great constructivist of Revolution. It organizes the language, it cuts out the new figures of speech, it maximizes the poetic jargon of Revolution.

The verse of Maiakovskii could be regarded as a poetically amplified telegraphic jargon. His verse is visually organized in special figures and constructions. It resembles a bulletin board with roughly pinned down commands, imperatives, announcements, assignments. It resembles a rail assembled for the revolutionary word-engine. It is a sheet of steel with words welded on it which the Poet casts into the public space. The revolutionary leaflets replaced the sacramental tablets

The telegraph was the machine pen of Revolution. It made possible the aesthetics of *maximal exhaustion* (Maiakovskii) of the creative force. "Me myself"—this is the autobiography of Maiakovskii. It has the form of a revolutionary CV, of a autoreport made by using a telegraph. It is a confession mutated into series of short, quick, articulate declarations that constitute the rhetoric of report and announce the commitment of the confessee to the Revolution.

## TELE-ICONO-GRAPH: LETTERS AND ARTS EX MACHINA

*The Revolution did not annul any of its achievements.*
*It increased the force of its achievements through material and technical forces. The book will annihilate the tribune. In its time, the book did annihilate the handwritten manuscript. The manuscript is only a beginning of a book. The tribune and the public platform will be carried forward and expanded by the radio. The radio—that is a further advancement of the word, of the slogan, of poetry. The revolution gave us the audible word, audible poetry.*
                    Maiakovskii (Lawton 1988, 263)

The rhetoric of the telegraph affected and was affected by the general revolutionary iconographia. The prodigious appearance of the Revolution was generated in the camera. The movie or the moving vision cut out by the machine and projected on the screen had the same speed and shocking rhetoric. Mechanically accelerated Icon had the same constructive principle as Maiakovskii's verse. Launching visions into life by means of the camera-catapult demonstrates the same revolutionary strategy as the telegraphic language does.

Both the telegraph and the iconograph (shooting and projecting apparatus) were the new speed assembly lines where the linguistic and the visual elements of Revolution were fit together. The grammar is the same—to produce shocking and politically appointed linguistic or visual devices. The artful work of the speed mechanisms caused an enormous acceleration in society pushing it towards its futuristic perfection and integrity.

According to Eisenstein, Attraction "is every aggressive moment... which acts upon the spectator's senses or psyche, an effect which is experimentally verified and mathematically calculated with a view to causing definite emotional shocks in the perceiver; which makes possible the perception of the idea of the things demonstrated, the final ideological conclusion."

Eisenstein's idea about the montage of attractions as the new iconographic principle of the cinematograph is, in fact, the same principle already manifested in the telegraphic verse of Maiakovskii. By assembling pieces of revolutionary reality—objects, names, visions—to create a new tough poetic construction which agitates for and propagates Revolution.

The new poetics is assigned by the Revolution to reorganize the structure of the psyche, to stimulate a sharp perception in the new agent of history (the proletariat), to push the consciousness of the masses into the battlefield of the political interests.

Art has a political assignment. It leads consciousness to the predesigned ideological conclusion—the Last ideological Judgment.

**ART AND FACT:**

**THE VIRTUAL REALITY OF THE REVOLUTION**

*Work represents for us not an aesthetic goal-in-itself,*
*but a laboratory for the best articulation of contempo-*
*rary facts.*
> *Maiakovskii and Brik (Stephan 1981, 98)*

In order to become a fact, an event should be broadcast through the channels and the speed lines of the media. It should be mediated in order to acquire virtual reality. It should acquire publicity and political actuality through the new administrative language of the Revolution. The fact is an event transformed into a political *attraction,* charged with ideological significance, accelerated to the utmost and launched into the public space by means of telegraphic and iconographic apparatuses.

Art manufactures facts. Art turns the empirical reality of Revolution into an outstanding and suggestive aggregate of facts. Art produces the virtual reality of the revolution. Art provides revolutionary turbulence with political design and premeditation. It makes Revolution visible. Art is the ideological conclusion of the empirical flux of the Revolution.

Revolution plus facts-manufacture and acceleration: that is Art.

### AGIT-PROP ACADEMY OF THE ARTS

*Our weapon is model, agitation and propaganda.*
> *LEF (Brodskii et al. 1929, 235)*

*Assignment instead of content.*
> *Tretiakov (Brodskii et al. 1929, 238)*

Revolutionary ideology is elaborated into universal science because its concepts are originally fabricated and tested as metaphors and icons in the agit-prop guilds of the arts.

Agit-prop invents stunning fortifications for the Left Front. The system of agit-prop brigades has different detachments following different assignments—theory of device, visual device, verse device and divisions for constructors, for workers, for directors, for Party design of life, and so on. It is an academy, a laboratory and a workshop in one.

Agit-prop lab accelerates class consciousness to the point of a miracle. The agit-prop becomes the headquarters of LEF with a clear-cut mission—to educate the masses, to accelerate the class consciousness and to stimulate self-awareness of the historical moment, to launch campaigns against obscurantism.

Chemistry, for instance, as modern science was abstracted from alchemy. From the figurative turbulence of the magic signs and compounds was extracted the purity of a science.

Inversely, a scientific concept, in order to function as a weapon of the Left Front, needs to be transformed into a blasting metaphor. Some poetic devices, manufactured by agit-prop, are concepts borrowed from science and recharged for the purpose of the Revolution.

### THE POLITICAL LABORATORY

*Experiment with a march-like structure in order to organize the revolutionary turmoil.*
> *Tretiakov (Stephan 1981, 99)*

*A treaty between LEF and MAPP:*

*Both sides agree:*

*Without interrupting the laboratory work to direct all
creative activity towards organization of the reader's
psyche and consciousness according the communist targets of the proletariat.*
(Brodskii et al. 1929, 246)

It is explicitly declared in the programs of LEF that the work of art is a
laboratory where the future forms of life are worked out, experimented,
tested and glorified. It is there that the weapons and the devices are assembled by the help of which the Left Front moves forward and the limits of art are pushed forward. Thus the territory of Revolution expands.

The verbal armor of the Teaching is forged in the laboratory. The
ideas are objectivized as revolutionary badges one wears on one's lapel
when marching in the ranks of the Revolution. The badges of revolution
are molded by agit-prop art. A wave of badges with revolutionary symbols engraved on them, and revolutionary slogans imprinted on them,
overwhelmed life. The badge *(znachok)* is a special sign *(znak)* borne by
the Revolution, charged with a suggestive political significance *(znache-
nie)* and a demonstrative propaganda assignment *(na-znachenie)*.

The agit-prop manufactory has designed and produced series of
conceptual badges. The major revolutionary symbols and figures are
engraved on them. These badges propagate the revolutionary imagery
but first and foremost various suggestive figures of Lenin. These are the
ornamental miniatures of the grand communist conception of the new
world. People wear them on their lapels, distribute them around, and
these disseminate revolutionary concepts and icons. The badges
sharpen people's awareness of communism and keep class consciousness vigilant against the bourgeois viruses that would spoil the proletarian vision. These badges impregnate the microstructures of everyday
consciousness and expand the circuit of the "universal connection" of
communism down in the lower depths, in the most diversified zone of
life. These are the smallest meaningful units of communism, tokens that
signify and assign communism to the people.

In the spring of 1991 I happened to be in Vienna and visited the exhibition of Russian constructivism (Rodchenko and Stepanova) which
had opened shortly before. There I found red amazing exhibit. It was a
small candy box with a constructivist label that said: "Buy this caramel,
which will make the Red Star shine." Thus a magic connection was established between the profane, everyday act of purchasing a caramel
and the sacred shine of the revolutionary sacraments, inviolable sym-

bols and objects impregnated with proletarian consciousness. The caramel was hereby advertised not as healthy and nutritious but as a politically efficient product. You buy it, and thus you keep the Revolution shining in the mind. You suck on it and thus you charge the battery of Revolution. Through the simplest everyday activities people communicate with the sublime and propagate Revolution. Thus the "universal connection" of communism was established between all things, names and acts.

Let us go back to the beginning of the Western metaphysics and compare the revolutionary hierarchy of images and representations with the one built by Plato in his allegorical Cave. There are three main stages of abstraction and purification of vision, and three figures manifest them: *Idols*—mortal corporeality and changing appearances grow together and diversify life; *Icons*—the appearances are abstracted from corporality, conceptualized and idealized despite the diverse bodies that could possibly materialize them; *Ideas*—there are neither appearances nor bodies but rather a pure *paradigm* that emerges through contemplation of the mind. Vision ascends, crossing a polluted realm where only diversities of bodies and appearances proliferate, and then enters the radiant realm of universal Ideas.

Agit-prop builds a different, in a sense inverted, hierarchy. Generated by the pure Ideas and abstractions of the Teaching that awaken class consciousness, proletarian vision enters the realm of Party concretized signification—badges-signifiers, conceptual icons, directives and slogans. Finally it descends down there in the virtual "Cave" to see the Idol—the mummy which immediately radiates communism.

What metaphysics enacts as pure Being—the paradigm which is representable only through pure contemplation of ideas and provokes insight, communism poses as Idol—the mummy incarnate of the doctrine that provokes paranoia. Phantoms and shadows acquired bodies, appearances were made identities. The ultimate Other—the Corpse was radically familiarized.

## ENGINEERING THE PSYCHE

*The worker of Art must become psycho-engineer, psycho-constructor.*
*Tretiakov (Brodskii et al. 1929, 242)*

Psyche is a special membrane, an extremely sensitive tissue of nerve synapses and endings which transforms the elemental resources of the revolution into individual power and spiritual integrity. The worker of the agit-prop lab makes the psychic membrane of the masses resound with revolution. Thus Left Front line expands in the territory of the psychic and chases away the bourgeois ideologies who tamper with the consciousness of the masses. The artist is charged to keep a constant watch for bourgeois sabotage lest it disorders the Left Front of the psychic. For this purpose agit-prop impregnates the psyche of the masses with symbols of class interest.

### THE GRANITE PILLOW

*We, the communists, are people of a special make. We*
*are made of a special material.*

*Stalin*

It is said that Maiakovskii used to sleep on a stone instead of a pillow in order to train his body and his dreams to acquire the features of the future human corporality.

A revolutionary used to sleep on a board with nails, Maiakovskii—on a grave stone instead of bed in order to overcome the fear of death. The grave is the future bed of the body and the body should not be scared of it; even, it has to experience an overwhelming longing toward its future. Through the funereal exercise the body is penetrated by the stone might of its future bed. The body memorizes its own future resting on the grave memorial.

Revolution is an ordeal for the human physique. The mortal corporeality should be trained and solidified in order to endure the ultimate strain in the time of Revolution. Maiakovskii trained himself to be a citizen of the future, to resist death by having a stonelike body, to testify to the future by the properties of his body.

This was Maiakovskii as he was said to be—not just a craftsman cutting out the word according to a modernistic pattern, but a body that suffers the same modernization as the verse itself.

*I do not belong to the group of worshippers of this kind*
*of poetic talent (Maiakovskii's), although I fully appreci-*
*ate my incompetence in that field, but I have not for*
*ages experienced such a pleasure from a political and ad-*
*ministrative perspective.*

*Lenin (LEF AGITKI 1925, 9)*

# 2

# Revolutionary Merger of Science and Art

Radical leftist modernism believes implicitly in constructive rationality, which has overcome bourgeois prejudices and developed its own bold visions in the industrial spaces. The political geometric mind is the genius of modernization and finds its final justification in science. Each action of the new agent of history, the proletariat, is constructively and scientifically guaranteed in advance in the clear spaces of political geometrism. It is here that the utopia of modernism arises. When the concepts of any scientific field are deliberately generalized and made to solve global problems, they turn into metaphors. They turn into crevices, through which gapes the wonderful view of a brand-new world. Such an amplification of the scientific concept into a world-building metaphor, into a mythical poetic figure, is a political manipulation. To be precise, it is a propaganda manipulation of a political plot for a total and radical world-modernization.

The concept as an instrument of scientific theory is usurped by the actual political design and comes to be used as a metaphor. It becomes pregnant with revolution. That is exactly what was done to the critical spirit of Marxism. That is what was done to the scientific laboratories, whose poetic glorification made possible the mass experiments over immense areas of the earth.

Science justifies all. The politically perfect world is the one which can be scientifically justified. Modern art builds just such a world. In this sense, modern art is science turned into a work-world.

## THE RED GEOMETRIST

Man invents and produces ever finer and more perfect implements. Man constantly reduces their size and thus achieves great technological and social results. These implements make man move ever faster and more precise. They enable man to master the world and push man to the limits of his corporal being. Propped up by these wonderful prostheses, man surpasses his earthly limitations and enters the spheres of an omnipotent inventive rationality. Art is a sublime organizational condition of those prostheses.

Russian proletarian art, that is, political art, is in a decisive struggle with the irrational Russian soul, with the forces of its sobbing sentimentality. Proletarian political constructivism introduces the Nordic spirit of the geometrical mind.

The red specter of communism becomes the Geometrist of the new age, the greatest Constructivist and political Dadaist. This Geometrist invented and produced unprecedented prostheses which would release the laboring body and would throw it into the community of radiant comradeship.

## THE BODY-AGGREGATE

*I am kino-eye. I am a builder.*
*I create a man more perfect than Adam, I create*
*thousands of different people in accordance with prelim*
*inary blueprints and diagrams of different kinds.*
*I am kino-eye.*
*From one person I take the hands, the strongest*
*and the most dexterous; from another I take the legs, the*
*swiftest and most shapely; from a third, the most beauti-*
*ful and expressive head—and through montage I create*
*a new, perfect man.*
Dziga Vertov (1984, 17)

A modern commune does not come together on a congregational basis, that is, on the principle of religious faith and initiation. It is built up on "aggregational" basis. The future collective body is represented as an electrified machinelike aggregate. This body, as an aggregate, cannot be described. The descriptive line (discourse) is helpless in this case. That is why the constructivists and the Dadaists repudiate descriptive lines (discourses), because they have no political constructivist potentialities and power. Such a power has only planning, designing lines. Because of that, the body of the new political agent, the proletariat, can be neither drawn nor described. It can only be designed, tailored and assembled. The red Geometrist designs and cuts out the body-aggregate of the proletariat using special tailoring machines like the film camera and scissors

## DISCIPLINING OF THE MASS MAN

*The Futurists make it possible for the masses to become*
*complete masters of their language.*
Tretiakov (Lawton 1988, 245)

If we attempt to reconstruct the modernist project from the start of this century, we would see that it owes its political aesthetic radicalism to the imperative—"Here and now replace this world with a new one!" That presupposes two things—invention, design of the new unity of the world, and the disciplining of an agent, or rather an actor, who would erect it. The new unity of the world and the athletic capability of the Erector—these are prerequisites for the project. What remains to be done is for the action itself to happen to us here, now, immediately. This action is the modernist act of genius which will be achieved not by that degraded bourgeois personage the Artist, or by a senile, exhausted God. The decisive act of genius is achieved by the Mass Man. His communal body accomplishes a radical feat of labor by erecting the final work— the New World.

Apparently, the political order of this New World is designed as a work ultimately open, encompassing in its space the body of its creator. The creator moves into his creation. This waste-free act of creation leaves nothing behind itself or outside itself, which with its sick body could inflame the new flesh of the world.

The suitability of the modernist project to life is guaranteed by an already completed rational act, which aspires to the high status of being scientific. The project is scientifically thought out and proven. The designing of the new world is based on the cool-minded Geometrist—the predecessor of scientific communism. The heat arises only later in the communal body of the Mass Man, who will make the effort of the construction itself. The modernist manifesto calls for immediate mass action. In this sense, behind the manifesto lies the cool mind of the modernist designer, and after it must be brought out the creative Mass Body. The manifesto is framed by a scientific mind and an artistic creation. Before is the political design, after is the new political order of the world. It might be said that the manifesto is the third position, which stands between the scientifically worked out normative poetics and the concrete work created in accordance with it. In the manifesto, scientific and artistic, political and aesthetic discourses fuse. The scientific concept and the poetical metaphor merge in the imperative form of manifesto. And so began the grand construction of scientifically proved metaphors, that is, imperatives were realized.

The only thing that has been accomplished after the calls of Dada and of scientific communism is the Party procedure of disciplining Mass Man. The creation of a new world did not take place, because the body refused to accept the communal state as its own creative state. The totalitarian state came to discipline a Mass Body, but it failed and it could not "wither away," as predicted by scientific communism.

When speaking of the "old world" one may say that bourgeois society has transformed the social bodies into organs of the personal, the one-sided and peculiar. Bourgeois space rests on the principle of heterogenia because by virtue of its definitions every body is alien to all others. Bourgeois democracy creates a political order capable of governing the segmented social space and enabling the communication of the alien bodies. Bourgeois law regulates the possible concord, accordance and togetherness of the heterogeneous bodies. It organizes into a community the individuals that occupy a different place in society. According to this juridical principle, no physical body may exist out-side the law or above it. The law acts equally both on the body of the President and the Dadaist. In contrast to this the bodies are entitled to differ with respect to their property, interests, physiognomy and choice. Equivalent social relations are introduced and ruled by mediators, such as money, alienated from the bodies. Precisely money enables the expression and realization of the actual differences between the separate bodies and their peculiar intercourse in the common space of the market.

And conversely, in order to create a Mass Man, it is necessary to liquidate all attributes, procedures and principles which identify the bodies as particular and one-sided, as personal entities in a common space. In this case, equivalence will not be ensured by alienated mediators such as money, but by the physical bodies of the subjects of the new communal world. Thus they become equal and Homo-genius, which makes possible the act of a great construction that involves a maximum of mass participation and ultimately welds the bodies together. The communal body consists of fragments that have an equal stake in the common entity and an equal interest in everything beyond their physical limits. Thus money is rendered superfluous, and so is the right to be different and so is the state as an institution which protects the differences. What remains is the body of the Mass Man, left alone with his own will, which draws strength from his primal natural drives: to eat, to copulate, to be in a well-lit and warm place.

An interesting example of Mass Man utopia are the ideas of Bogdanov, that vigorous ideologist of the most outspoken political art in Russia—the Proletcult. This art was suffocated by Lenin because it did not give in to Bolshevization and did not conform to Party interests. The political modernism of Bogdanov became harmful, because Lenin had already turned the political idea into a Party idea and the proletariat had to build not a world, but a Party. Bogdanov charged the proletariat with ontological interests. Lenin charged it with ideological ones. Modernization as the meaning of political art manifests intuitions of a world. Ideology as the meaning of Party art manifests intuitions of a power.


Up until now the major concern of this book was the invention and use of various revolutionary devices, apparatus, appliances, gear and the way artists operate with them and cut out a new reality. From now on we will direct our attention to planning and establishing centers for mass-scale modernization of human consciousness and physique, for a scientifically justified social engineering. We will examine various projects that enact the spaces of the bright future—the new cities, together with numerous bold visions for a universal perfection of man achieved through abolishing gender, class and mental differences and launching humans in the outer space for final reunion and eternal life.


## THE PLOT OF MODERNISM AND ITS CENTERS

*Sie haben eine Welt zu gewinnen*
*Manifest der kommunistischen Partei*
             *Marx and Engels*


### THE CENTER WHICH UNITES THE CLASS

It was Bogdanov the author of the "organizational theory" of society, who worked out various visions and metaphors for the role and place of the new proletarian art which captivate the mass consciousness even now. Art, he said, is the higher organization of the social experience, the most powerful means for the concentration of the collective forces of the new class. Art is a perfect organization of the class struggle. It is a radically collectivized labor. In it the notion of private property and personality cannot exist. It is a supreme stage of mass proletarian labor.

Modernized mind controls the body through designing and mastering prostheses—of all those machines, transmissions, apparatuses and automata that make body superable and take over its dark, knotty irrationality.

Modern large-scale industry is turned into a gymnastic platform with futuristic apparatus assembled on it where proletarian art demonstrates its stunning "attractions" (Eisenstein), its grotesque "bio-mechanics" (Meyerhold). All of this rests on the scientific justification of modern technology and automation. Here originates the principle of the creative mass force engaged in this process: *comradeship.* The collectivism of the proletarians homogenizes their social interest. It unifies them and sensitizes them to all things alien, to all things bourgeois. Comradeship does not arise from religious love, but from the technological togetherness of bodies in the process of labor. Comradeship springs from the new geometrical mode of life. The human corporality must become the immediate substance of comradeship. That is why the proletarian body of the new class must be united through a common substance.

For Bogdanov, blood is the very substance which should be exchanged between comrades and thus comradeship will flow directly into the bodies of the proletarians. He founded the first blood transfusion clinic, only not with a medical but with an immediately political purpose. Science thus directly begins serving politics, or to be more exact, directly grows into politics. Blood transfusion as the subject of science becomes a means for homogenizing a united collective political agent: the proletariat.

Brotherhood solidified through blood fusion is an ancient ritual which is charged with enormous symbolic power. This sacred act, which has its cause in the poetic/mythical constitution of the world, becomes an instrument of science and is conducted through a sheer medical procedures ideologically justified and practiced on a mass scale.

This took the life of Bogdanov, himself. He exchanged blood with a man with whom he was totally incompatible. He failed to survive through the antagonism of the alien blood and died. The attempt to produce a purely communal body ended with death. Dada also dreams of such a body and such a center —not only for blood, but also for sex (sperm): see Dada manifesto below.

## MODERNIZATION OF THE HUMAN CORPORALITY

### Ideology and Genitals

*According to Ermilov, the "harmonious man" would
maintain equilibrium between "psyche and ideology,"
between "instinct and consciousness," between "the
conscious and the subconscious." Ideas acquired
through conscious effort would penetrate and become
one with the subconscious and the instinctive. Upon
reaching this stage of development, a man could manifest his ideology spontaneously by an unconditioned reflex. When the right ideology had entered the "psycho"
of the masses, the cultural revolution would be accomplished and Russia would then be a socialist country.*
*Ermolaev (1977, 61–62)*

We hit here one of the most far reaching strategies of political modernism, namely: ideo-logos realized as physio-logos! Ideology has to penetrate the unconditional nature of physiology and its basic instinct. Revolutionary ideology is expected to set the biological motor and thus to mobilize the primal functions of the human organism. Ideology impregnates human corporality with class self-consciousness and thus makes it proof against decay.

Communist ideology conducts the class interest in the realm of proletarian consciousness, while the bourgeois ideology obscures the interest that it stands for. And Red ideology will transgress the limit of consciousness itself growing ultimately into the proletarian physiology. There it starts tempering with and conditioning the basic reflex. Red ideology is not a bare superstructure that hovers around the basis of social reality as its rival does. It penetrates the very human fabric and resets its unconditional set-up. Thus it is set to change the constitution of the very human physique by building a proletarian proper body which possesses unprecedented faculties and is capable of performing miracles on earth. Ideology becomes an inherent property of the body. Ideology penetrates the genitals. The copulation disseminates ideology.

The director Meyerhold and the artist Lisitskii staged in 1928 *I Want a Child*, a play written by Sergei Tretiakov. This team of authors was apparently influenced by the idea of a eugenic selection of a sound constituency for the new world and a purification of its class essence by matching the most sound representatives. The theater critic Konstantin Rudnitskii (1981, 437–38) abstracts the ideological point of this radical Left-Front performance:

> The idea of the play is strikingly simple. The construction of the new world requires physically perfect and ideologically healthy cadres. Therefore, it is equally criminal to "waste sexual energy" and to bear children of men selected by the caprices of love. Healthy, strong, whole woman of proletarian background must mate with healthy worker males. "The State," said one of the heroes of this play, the Disciplinarian, "encourages such selection" in consequence of which "a new breed of people" appears. He warned that "for all the sickly and the sexual wastrels" the "day of frightful fasting" was coming. Love, according to this program, was not totally eliminated, but was put off until better times. "When the human species is uplifted, you can love all you like, but for now, take it easy."
>
> It was with accordance with this program that the heroine of the play, the young Latvian Communist woman Milda Grignau, organized her personal life. This strong, healthy lass invited a worker—Yakov the construction worker—to her room and asked him a number of form questions (such as whether there were any illness or, God forbid, foreign admixtures in his background). "Comrade, I want to have a child," Milda informed her selected one, "but I want a good child, I want his father to be a working man." After this, the heroine, not without difficulty, persuaded the astonished fellow to cohabit with her and then bore a child . . . when Milda became pregnant she decisively re-

fused any further services from her partner: the job was done, there was no point for any further waste of sexual energy.

## The New/Old Doctrine

*The doctrine of formation is the doctrine of
transformation.*
                         Goethe (1952, 13)

We are going to turn now to what is probably the most ambitious goal of the modernist project since the turn of the century for inventing of a new unprecedented political condition and physique of the human body situated in the world of the future. The plan for the construction of the new revolutionary world has received considerable attention from scholars. In contrast, the physiology of the inhabitant of this world is often unappreciated or even neglected, while the project elaborates it with a great precision. The new space of the world needs a new human body capable of living in it. The new world would be empty if not populated by people with a special physique. A Man with a special corporal makeup—this is major concern of the project. The present man would be completely disabled if let into the new world. The present man is obsolescent.

For this investigation the very term *modernist project* indicates a secondary sketch abstracted from numerous political utopian projects for radical change in the nature of the human being and the construction of the world it inhabits—failed projects for the solution of the earthly anatomical, political, sexual problems.

### PROJECTION OF THE VEGETAL SEX

*The Ur-plant as I see it will be the most wonderful creation in the whole world, and nature herself will envy me for it. With this model and the key to it, one will be able to invent plants without limit to conform, that is to say, plants which even if they do not actually exist nevertheless might exist and which are not merely picturesque or poetic visions and illusions, but have inner truth and logic. The same law will permit itself to be applied to everything that is living.*
                         Goethe to Herder (1952, 14)

How will the new physical, sexual and political good be conquered? This is the general question for the modernist project. Not just the world must be radically changed, but the body-being of its inhabitants. For this purpose, a new trans-zoomorphous body must be designed which has vegetal features and a biomechanical principle of action. This is a body that can be technologically improved in the laboratories.

Why should a vegetal body that has centralized vital functions directed by an external brain-center be developed and glorified as the new blissful human condition? This is the general question we should answer. Four cases of body modernization are selected here to elaborate on. Probably some of them do not have any direct historical relation, although they stand for one and same Godlike end of modern times—a new world with a new creature in it to be created.

Let us start with the most important political manifesto of Berlin Dadaism decreeing the new communist system and its constitution. Then comes Wilchelm Reich and his elaborate idea of a new sexual politics, known as Sex-Pol, and the sexual revolution of the unbound orgasm. Then we are going to review a Russian religious philosopher who located his utopian society in outer space, and not on an unknown island on the earth, which indicates a crucial shift in the classical utopian localization of the model society. Finally, we are going to consider a vision of building a transsexual body that transgresses the limitations of the original Adam sexual constitution followed by a mass-scale resurrection of the dead.

## A Dada Manifesto

WHAT IS DADAISM AND WHAT DOES IT WANT
IN GERMANY?
1.   *Dadaism demands:*
  1)   *The international revolutionary union of all
        creative and intellectual men and women on
        the basis of radical Communism;*
  2)   *The introduction of progressive unemployment
        through comprehensive mechanization of every
        field of activity. Only by unemployment does
        it become possible for the individual to achieve
        certainty as to the truth of life and finally be-
        come accustomed to experience;*
  3)   *The immediate expropriation of property (so-
        cialization) and the communal feeding of all;
        further, the erection of cities of light, and gar-
        dens which will belong to society as a whole
        and prepare man for a state of freedom.*
2.   *The Central Council demands:*
  a)   *Daily meals at public expense for all creative
        and intellectual men and women on the Pots-
        damer Platz (Berlin);*

    *b)  Compulsory adherence of all clergymen and*
        *teachers to the Dadaist articles of faith;*
    *c)  The most brutal struggle against all directions*
        *of so-called "workers of the spirit" (Hiller,*
        *Adler), against their concealed bourgeoism,*
        *against expressionism, and post-classical edu-*
        *cation as advocated by the Sturm group;*
    *d)  The immediate erection of a state art center,*
        *elimination of concepts of property in the new*
        *art (expressionism); the concept of property is*
        *entirely excluded from the super-individual*
        *movement of Dadaism which liberates all*
        *mankind;*
    *e)  Introduction of the simultaneous poem as a*
        *Communist state prayer;*
    *f)  Requisition of churches for the performance of*
        *bruitism simultaneous and Dadaist poems;*
    *g)  Establishment of a Dadaist advisory council for*
        *the remodeling of life in every city of over*
        *50,000 inhabitants;*
    *h)  Immediate organization of a large scale Dadaist*
        *propaganda campaign with 150 circuses for the*
        *enlightenment of the proletariat;*
    *i)  Submission of all laws and decrees to the*
        *Dadaist central council for approval;*
    *j)  Immediate regulation of all sexual relations*
        *according to the views of international*
        *Dadaism through establishment of a Dadaist*
        *sexual center.*

    *The Dadaist revolutionary central council. German group: Hausmann, Huelsenbeck Business office: Charlottenburg, Kantstrasse 118. Applications for membership taken at business office.*

            *(Motherwell and Flam 1981, 41–42)*

So we see that the political order of the new world is designed as a work ultimately open, encompassing in its space the body of its creator. The creator moves into his creation.

This manifesto is a perfect example of modernistic coalescence of a political and an aesthetic project for radical change and in this sense is an excellent example of Dada's political aesthetics. It offers the following procedures for the disciplined ordering of the communal body into the organizational patterns of the new world.

1. Complete discharge of the bodies from all kinds of professional operations through mechanization of labor. In the old world bodies are agents of social differences. The replacement of bodies with machines

in the sphere of social and professional division resolves the problem since the machines take over the differences the bodies have been standing for.

2. Expropriation of property. The various forms and contents of property, the various fashions of ownership justifies the heterogeneity of the bodies and their possible interaction with the other bodies. This rules the "I" versus the "Others" opposition. The identity of the "I" as different from any "Other" is ensured by these two principles of action and property.

3. Assembling sun cities and garden cities, that is, communal spaces as grand works populated by their own builders. That will expose the bodies to the shaft of all-pervading eternal illumination and insolation. The bodies absorb light and no longer cast any shadows; they are no longer prone to ghostly splitting caused by the forces of darkness in them.

The sun city is an eternal sun trap organized on the Earth's crust where the bodies overcome their cave zoomorphism and become heliotropes. In the garden city vegetation is imposed as a principle of the communal body.

Vegetation is sexless. Exposed to this communal sun trap, man turns into a plant, his body becomes a stem which processes sunlight by means of photosynthesis and in this way gets rid of the dark forces of the sexual drive. This is why the sun city and the garden city are actually one. In this city the body-stems get comradely attached to each other and sink into the apathetic process of vegetative hybridization/parthenogenesis instead of tearing each other apart by ecstatic embraces. Copulation is replaced by the crossing of twigs in the crown of the tree called Mass Man.

4. Public feeding of the bodies. This concerns the public photosynthesis of the vegetating communal body. Feeding and copulation—these two actions which play a most important role in any mythical, magical, religious or secular culture—are deprived of their zoomorphism because at any time they may let animalistic chaos into the Garden. The ultimate triumph of the beast over its pray is the moment when it devours it. This is why every culture charges with great significance the acts of hunting, preparing the food, eating and mastication, and has them caught in a net of rituals and ceremonies in order to tame them. It is in this publicly ritualized delay and prolongation of feeding that the oral expansion of the animal gets exhausted. In the garden-sun city drives do not exist to be exhausted. The vegetative metamorphosis of the communal body deprives it of its original urge to bite, to swallow and to pounce. The plant does not swallow bodies but absorbs light; it

does not pounce, it attaches itself. As a result of this general metamorphosis, the bones get soft; the teeth and the claws, those blades that tear apart the other's body, fall out. The calcified edges of the beast become mushy and load it down like thick teardrops. The beast degenerates into a publicly tear-shedding stem exposed to eternal insolation.

5. Bruitism introduced in the churches as official state prayer. Bruitism literary means "making noise." Turned into a Mass Man, Dada makes the biggest possible noise in its temples. By chanting its Dadaist abracadabra it dispenses with language—one of the most powerful instruments for imposing differences. Language diversifies life, expresses the heterogeneous interests of the bodies, personalizes the speaking subject by means of style and the form of expression. Conversely, the language manifestations of the communal body are the roar of the abracadabra. The eloquence of this body is the sharpest noise it can make. Noise homogenizes its sources. For this reason it is the sole way of coping with the Babylonian disintegration of language. Noise welds the communal body so that it becomes capable of accomplishing this once-frustrated labor feat of erecting the Tower of the new world.

I can imagine it: The Tower of Babel is finally erected. Thus it could be a perfect prison for mankind. It should be a fortified erection of the maximum Power. In its completeness the social order will be the final one, the language will be the final one. Man will be batch produced as perfect "ready-made-subject." This would be the Tower of uniformity. It would be the final "ready-made-object" itself.

The reality opposite to the Tower is Babel: a collage of incompatible realities, languages, gestures which repel and assault each other. Through Babel the Tower as a complete work is made impossible. The crash of the already fragmented languages demolishes the Monolith and disseminates around the world the ruins as monuments of the Dadaist endeavor of God.

The diaspora of languages is manifested as feverish babble. The babble is a kind of bruitism which cannot be understood but only heard. The babble represents the crash of the falling Tower.

6. The manifesto enacts the presence of a superior political body—Central Dadaist Council of the World Revolution (CDCWR) placed above the laws and regulations so that it can control and supervise them. This body should be detached from the rules and routines which regulate the communication and association of the various social bodies. The CDCWR stands untouchable above the active differences. This superior political body initiates the social order without being subject to it. It is charged with the only power that can possibly turn bourgeois zoomorphism into a vegetal commune. The CDCWR is a superior veg-

etable which replaces the imperialist genitals of society. It enmeshes the bodies and in this way represses the urge for erotic penetration.

7. The manifesto ends with appeal for establishment of a Dadaist Sexual Center; with the radical centralization and concentration of the sexual power. It has been repressively derived from the bodies; made state property and exhausted according to a central planning. "The sexual power for political purposes!" with this slogan the Sexual Center castrates the zoological body. The collective libido is safeguarded in the batteries of the center.

We were not living in the garden-city. We were the plants in it. In the vegetal colony.[1]

## The Sex-Pol Accumulators of Wilhelm Reich

*Sex life is not a private affair . . . it interferes with the*
*political struggle.*
                        *Wilhelm Reich (1972, 254)*

The question of the Sexual Center which was discussed above is still open. To what extent is it a sufficiently rationalized notion of the future organization of society, or perhaps just a "bold metaphor," a rhetorical cutting edge sharpened for political purposes? This question will always remain open if the problems of sex and eroticism are not analyzed within the broader context of the century in order to reconstruct the utopian type of sexual organization of a communal society.

Sexuality was an issue for the racial theory of Nazism and for the class theory of Bolshevism. In the former it was encouraged as a sublime form of racial exultation and demographic expansion, while in the latter it was subjected to total repression because the basis of communal society was not sought in the racial but in the class properties of the body. Genetics and sexual theory were repressed by the "class-party ideology," the supremacy of which they threatened. The sexualization of the body under Nazism and its sterilization under Bolshevism stem from different political ideologies designed to proclaim and empower the supremacy of the communal body: the communal-racial or communal-class body.

1.  *Theory of the New Biology*—this is the title of a popular book published in Russia 1922 by E. Enchmen. The author of the book advances to the extreme the idea that psyche, mind, ideology are bourgeois nonsense and apparitions. The human being of the future will have biological passport issued by the *Revolutionary-Scientific Council of the World Commune* that identifies his/her physiological properties and reflects all its conditions including the "coefficient of joyfulness." This passport serves as a special coupon that regulates the regime of consumption and exhaustion of the new organism (50;40).

The problem of sexuality gained wide popularity with the advent of the ideas and practice of the so-called sexual revolution. Thus we face yet another revolution which again champions communal life, again claims to be based on science and again creates utopian structures through its ideology. I do not claim that the ideas of Reich, the ideologist of the sexual revolution, about orgone and the orgasm stand in any direct relationship with Dada and its Sexual Center. But it is important to note that a look at the general landscape of culture shows that in one place sexuality has provoked visions; in another, an ideology; in still another, ideology and practice; in a fourth place, a comprehensive structure of organized life for the masses; in a fifth, a single metaphor and so on. It is natural to concentrate our attention on the place where this issue is most extensively elaborated in terms of metaphors, in terms of concepts, as a science, as an ideology, as a practice, as a revolutionary action and as a new structure of life. I have in mind Wilhelm Reich and his work.

In contrast to the machinism of the nineteen twenties, Reich professed a radical deliverance from machine-prostheses and a recovery of the primal organicity of the body. Instead of mechanism he saw the organic as the savior of mankind. But let us take one thing at a time.

Reich was a disciple of Freud but he soon broke away from his teacher and Freud's fundamental concepts like "libido," "Oedipus complex" and the Freudian structure of the psyche. Reich generalized orgasm. The way of reaching orgasm was for him at the root of all human problems, all mental disorders, obsessions and frustrations. Reich preached that the orgasm marks the moment when the life energy attains or strives to attain a maximum potency in order to get completely exhausted. Because of this, any inability to attain that energy climax leads to regression and pathological "after-spending." Natural human existence was termed directly dependent on the ability to experience a complete orgasm. And Reich started clearing the way for orgasm.

The main obstacle on the way to the complete orgasm was the repressive function of the bourgeois personal character. The tough character was regarded highly by the bourgeois world. By bourgeois definition a character is complete when it is a unique constellation of features, when it is independent and strong-willed to the utmost. The character focuses *principium individuationis*. The character, that armada of imperatives, obsessive visions, compulsive autodisciplines, microdementia, idiosyncrasies and the like, was viewed by Reich as the autocrat which represses the complete spending of energy, the outpour of the orgasm. That is why the rigidly structured private bourgeois world must be replaced by a commune where the disciplining of the "character-armor" is impossible because there the body is deprived of its own private world, of its partiality which can be selflessly defended and fortified. In the communal organization of life, sexual energy is spent freely and completely.

The sexual revolution, advanced by Reich, was meant to dismantle the privatized bourgeois world and to build a communal life. Reich believed that the "healthy person," the so-called genitalic character, is an attribute of the working class and not of the bourgeoisie, the aristocracy or the intelligentsia. This was so because the workers already exist as a consolidated body thanks to the concentration and organization of their labor in industry.

In 1928 Reich joined the Austrian Communist Party. In 1929 he visited Russia. His work *Dialectical Materialism and Psychoanalysis* was published in Moscow. He was full of hope that the Russian Revolution will evolve into a sexual revolution because of its proletarian-Bolshevik character, that is, "genitalic character." The revolution was contemplated as a revolt of the healthy ones against the sick ones which heals society. Alas, with respect to sexuality exactly the opposite happened.

In 1930 Reich founded in Berlin a German association for Proletarian Sexual Policies. The politicization of this issue was inevitable, even natural, insofar as the sexual interest of mankind was in this case identified as a class-proletarian interest. Unlike Freud, Reich politicized the problem of sexuality, which made him resort to generalizations (well known from "scientific communism") about the new communal order of society and the new centralized political government of the world's sexual energy. It is easy to see why in 1934 Reich got kicked out of the International Psychoanalytical Association. But his being kicked out of the Communist Party in 1933 is not so easy to explain. The immediate motive was that he bond the radical political action, its motivation and goal, to the campaigns of sexuality. During the twenties Dada was not condemned by the Communist Party for the same kind of extremism. But it must be noted that the year is 1933. This was, alas, a new period for the Communist Party. It was a period when the modernist radical visions of the future and excess of imagination were suppressed in the Soviet Union, the center of communism. Communism was already following a new line: not a political but a Party line. Reich was very late in adopting a left-radical political style. At this time, he was a latter-day Dadaist within the communist movement. But in spite of that he persisted in the same style.

Following Marx, Reich embarked on a critique of sexual economy, or more specifically, of the bourgeois sex economy. The social need for a sexual revolution was derived from the critique of the bourgeois authoritarian family, morality, piety, education, Puritanism and other institutions of this kind. Revolution would come to do away with the old institutions, to redistribute the sexual resources of society and reform the structure of their exhaustion. This was the scientific and precisely sex-economic justification of revolution.

Towards the end of his life Reich again got in trouble because of his attempt to realize his radical modernist project with a whole new set of key metaphors and visions. He was convinced that he had discovered the universal agent of sexual energy—orgon—and that he could extract it in special bubbles called bions. For this purpose storage batteries called orgon-boxes were constructed. They were intended to accumulate and isolate energy. At a special laboratory, let us call it a sexual center, the cosmic orgon-energy would be justly distributed, channeled and utilized. The very agent of life will be scientifically, judiciously and technologically directed.

Here again we face the modernistic impetus to objectivize such moral, ideological and mythopoetic metaphors as "love," "happiness" and "comradeship." These metaphors are materialized according to a central political design.

As he attempted to build and launch his sexual center, Reich was caught, so to say, red-handed, accused and tried for fraud and then diagnosed as a paranoiac. That is what happened with this belated Dada at the time when all modernist visions and projects were put down as paranoia.

## THE VERTICAL UTOPIA OF NIKOLAI FYODOROV

*Science is proved by art.*
>     N. Fyodorov

Nikolai Fyodorov, a Russian philosopher from the age of the great projects for the modernization of the world (the late nineteenth and early twentieth century), is associated with the so-called Russian cosmism. This is the ultimate universalization of the Russian idea, the Russian mission to organize an unprecedented new cosmic order which will save man from the blind forces and monstrous urges of his "heavy" earth-gravitating body, from the private bourgeois character of trivial existence, from criminal imagination and the aggressive drive of the flesh. It will save him from the curse of being mortal and the eternal captivity of "gravitation," from the fatal bondage to this planet which decomposes and feeds on the human body.

Fyodorov was a recluse and his principal work, *Philosophy of the Common Cause* (Fyodorov 1982), was published after his death. Within the context of Russian religious universalism, the term "common cause" implies several ideals: a sublime form of liturgical public life—

"liturgy" literally means public service; full realization of the Russian communal way of life—the so-called Domostroy which regulates the main relationship between father and son, Tzar and people, patriarch and society; a shift of utopian consciousness, from the "geographically horizontal" to the "cosmic vertical" principle, that is, a modernization of utopian imagination itself.

We will examine the essential terms of cosmic liturgy to describe Fyodorov's project on the construction of the cosmic congregational space which ultimately solves all human problems: physiology, religion, political power, science, aesthetics.

## The Project

*The idea in general is neither subjective nor objective, it is projective.*

N. Fyodorov (1982, 429)

*Project* is key term in the *Philosophy of the Common Cause.* The project demonstrates the immediate transition of metaphysical philosophical speculations into reality. It blends ideal and practice. Within the project, the distinction between logical notion and artistic metaphor is blurred because the project demonstrates an original imagination where there is no difference between knowledge and creation, cognition and conception.

Creation is practiced cognition. The project conjoins the abstract idea and the concrete blueprint of the new world. Scientific discovery, religious revelation and artistic vision merge within the project. Imperative, knowledge and invention become one projecting mind.

Projection rules out the rifts between man's rational, artistic and moral being. Moreover, the project excludes the fatal split between the *object* and the *subject* of the action (cause). The repression of the *subjecting* one and the resistance of the *ob-jecting* one vanish in the act of the *pro-jecting* one. The magic of projection is that the creating subject and the created object merge in one body-construct.

## The New Organism: Transformation of the Human Physique

*The essence of the organism that we have to work out for ourselves is self-defined. This organism is in itself a unity of knowledge and action; the nutrition of this organism is a creative and conscious process of the human being transforming the elementary cosmic substances into mineral ones, then into vegetal and at the end into living tissues. The organs of this organism will*

*be the very instruments by means of which the human
being will act under the circumstances on which the
vegetal and the animal life will depend. By means of
these organs will be created the aero- and ethero-nautic
methods making him/her able to move and extract from
space the universal materials for the construction of
his/her organism. The human being will then carry in
him/herself the history of scientific discoveries and the
course of progress; he/she will unite chemistry and
physics in one, i.e., the whole cosmology—not in the
form of an abstract image but in the form of a cosmic
apparatus enabling him/her to be a real cosmopolitan,
i.e. to be omnipresent; and human being then will be a
really enlightened creature.*

N. Fyodorov (1982, 405)

The human corporality vacillates between two extremes: earth, which bears divine punishment, and cosmos, which brings divine salvation. The earthly body is shaped from flesh and its problem is *anatomical*. But the future cosmic organism is in project and its problem is *technologically constructive*. The question is how to surmount anatomy. Fyodorov's project sets out to construct the new, cosmic, saved corporality. The cosmic transmutation of the earthly human body will solve its main problems—nutrition, sex and mortality.

The principal concern of the *project* is the invention of a blissful collective organism. The earthly constitution of the body has to be changed radically. For the purpose, new cosmic nutritional substances will be invented, along with a new structure of digestion. The cosmic transmutation of the body will overcome the zoomorphous nature and will implant vegetative organs in it. Thus the body becomes capable of feeding on, and accumulating the all-pervading cosmic substance: light. The flesh turns into a photosynthesizing biomass charged with light and warmth in special greenhouses in outer space.

Light and sunshine become a primary economic force possessed, consumed and reproduced by the new human organism. The worker and the machine which produces the cosmic resource (light) become one entity. The rift between labor, machine and commodity is eliminated as the economic process merges with the biological process of the human organism itself. Exploitation becomes impossible, and so does ownership. Nor is crime possible any more since its two main sources—social inequality and bestial aggressiveness—are obliterated. The modernized body is an unprecedented plant species which is not rooted in the ground. There is no distinction whatsoever between root, stem and blossom. It moves in outer space and is rooted solely in the flood of solar light.

The bodies of the forefathers buried in the earth and their spirits roaming the cosmos, reunite in this organism. The Earth no longer engulfs the bodies of the forefathers, nor does it pull down the bodies of their sons or contain an inferno that releases monstrous apparitions. The Earth is thoroughly purged and freed from the curse of being a prison for man. Human organism acquired the properties of the central cosmic substance. It becomes ultimately mobile, fast and light. The problem is how this organism will finally turn into light projection? It must be taken beyond gravitation and accelerated to the speed of light, thus turning into a photon. Humankind should be turned into a flux of photons, that is, into coherent concentrated light beams. Consequently, humankind must be beamed into outer space. For the purpose, the project envisages the construction of special apparatuses, machines and spaceships which should make the human body a plant soaring through the sky. Moreover, the project envisages the construction of dynamic "base-station-centers" in outer space—the new cities. The flying city is a special congregational space of the new human vegetative organisms: the City of Light.

## Speed as a Key Metaphor

Fyodorov reviews the historical evolution of handwriting: from the laborious writing of pictograms and hieroglyphs through Gothic characters to modern shorthand and stenography. Missile weapons have a similar history—from siege engines through gunpowder weapons to rapid-fire assault rifles.

The speed and the character of writing influence the ability of consciousness to picture and imagine the world. The world accelerates with the acceleration of writing, with the improvement of the media and information channels, of machines and apparatuses generating and transmitting the writing and its modernized signs.

Projection is a radically accelerated writing, an ultimately fast imagination within whose figure-projects logical notion and artistic metaphor lose their distinction. The science/art rift appears only in the low-speed range of projection (writing).

As is known, projection is a generation of light, shaping figures through light. It is the writing of the modern age. Light is the very matter of this kind of writing. The projection apparatus is the most sophisticated device for speed writing.

The hologram should be regarded as the crown of writing which evolved from pictorgrams. The hologram is a pictogram projected (unfolded) in space itself. The act of writing is ultimately accelerated. Chalk as the matter of writing is replaced by rays and beams of photons. The hologram is an ultimately modernized pictogram. Artistic skill and invented technology lose their distinction within it. The image is propelled into the real volume of the world and thus transformed into an absolute, perfect phantom.

A Space Center and Laboratory will house a projection apparatus which will project (launch) humankind into outer space as a giant hologram. Projection as the fastest writing makes what it depicts immediately visible in the space. Writing launches its own contents into space.

## The Space Center-Museum-Observatory

*The transition towards reality is an act of abolishing the
divorce between art and science.*
                              N. Fyodorov (1982, 566)

The problem is how to organize a space which will effect the merging of science and art, encompass the complete memory of humankind in a special system and be totally open to outer space so that it can carry out the expansion (projection) of humankind in the latter by inventing and testing various aerostats and spaceships. What does it look like, this Space Center from which humanity will proceed to colonize outer space in order to achieve the liturgy of its new cosmic congregational life?

The project regards architecture as the crown of the arts, and astronomy as the crown of sciences. To build the Space Center, humanity must attain an architectural organization of space, an "urban structure" which combines the figure and functionality of the church, laboratory, observatory, library, launching pad and factory for cosmic substances and spacecraft. Fyodorov calls this space a Museum.

The Museum must display the entire historical legacy of humanity, all material and spiritual culture, and classify it in a perfect catalogue. This Catalogue is somewhat like a databank organized with hard-and-fast rules, something like a cybernetic machine, a homogeneous organism, a brain. Thanks to this catalogue, humanity's collective brain can think strategically. The catalogue has a direct line to the Museum exhibits. It has a direct line to the laboratories and observatory which feed new data and exhibits into it. It has a line to the churches, the liturgical spaces of the Center where man's new cosmic spirituality and corporality is formed and the "patrofication"—the resurrection of forefathers in the son's cosmic fold— carried out The Oedipal guilt is surmounted because the son recreates the father, the family recreates its predecessor killed in the primordial past.

The catalogue is the brain tissue and structure, a cybernetic automaton which rules the liturgical communication of all bodies of the new world. It is a device through which the historical memory of humanity and its actuality are ultimately accelerated. From the viewpoint of the ultimate speed, they merge and the linear time is lost. Past and present proceed so fast simultaneously that the idea of future wholly disappears.

Such a nondistinction between science and art, astronomy and architecture, lends the work of art a special status, entrusting it with a special task. The work of art is an immanently complete cosmos, a sacral order; it makes the global cosmic order demonstratively visible and conceivable. Its structure is a model of the structure of the cosmos. In this sense, to create a work of art means to immediately create a project for a new world, to project. In Fyodorov's Museum, the work of art has the status of a laboratory which invents the new system of the world. The scientific intellect proves itself precisely in the work of art, that is, in the project, mock-up, laboratory, in that which turns science into reality.

Science invents, art manufactures the artificial organs—apparatuses, spacecraft, projectors through which the body realizes its cosmic transmutation.

Science acquires reality in art.

## The Three Global Stages of Cosmic Liturgy.

*The solar system must be turned into an economic force.*
                    N. Fyodorov (1982, 423)

*The global act* is represented as launching, ultimate acceleration and photon transmutation of human corporality by means of artificial organs and prostheses. The organic and the mechanical lose their distinction.

*The global organ* is represented as *oculus ex machina*. The eye is the organ which absorbs the light. Vision is the fastest action of which the human body is capable. The biomass of the eye and the structure of its activity are what the entire body should turn into. The observatory is a giant ocular apparatus bringing the abilities of the eye to unprecedented perfection.

The projection apparatus is an *oculus ex machina* which beams rays of light, images and pictograms in space. It is a jet-propelled eye-engine. The Eye transforms into a projecting observatory which lights up and supervises outer space. An observatory which launches and substantiates the human gaze in outer space.

It is not accidental that one of the central ideas of modernism is to transform the properties of the human eye, to increase the abilities of the gaze, to mechanize and automate vision, to retail and reassemble the visual. To modernize icono-graphy through photo-graphy. To modernize pictograms through holograms.

Modernism has transformed vision into a jet-propelled device that creates itself its own activator. It applies the principle of a missile or rocket in a vacuum which Tsiolkovskii (the other great cosmic visionary) discovered—the apparatus itself ejaculates the substance which propels it. The ship itself creates the sea it sails.

*Global space:* the Museum. The Museum contains human memory and a projective potential in an ultraorganized system. The Museum is a complete work of art launched right into the cosmos to become the cosmos itself. The global space has the features of a jet-propelled eye-rocket which has encapsulated humanity shortly before launching-projecting it into outer space.

## The Principle of the Vertical Utopia

*The organs of the human being and their disposition in
the body have not till now adjusted to its vertical pose" . . .
the process of giving birth is not natural to a being having taken a vertical position.
     The uprising of the sons expressed in their erected
bodies, caused by the death of the fathers, is tragic.*
                    N. Fyodorov (1982, 12; 526–17)

Marx and Engels are said to have transformed socialism from an utopia into a science, utopian socialism into scientific communism. However, the utopias "transformed" by Marxism into a science are radically different in character from Fyodorov's cosmic utopia.

Apart from constructing imaginary models of the world, utopias from the time of "early capitalism" fit the age of the great geographical discoveries, the age of Europe's horizontal expansion and colonization of the "New World." This caused the decline of the mythological cartography, changed the symbolic representation of territory with a political one and developed a new martial vision for expansion on the map that made the colonization possible.

Colonization is building a new world. When a civilization starts expanding, it creates imaginary models of society. Expansion presupposes mutations in the expanding social organism and this spawns visions of its integrity in a brand new system. In this sense, the utopia is an ideological construct of the expansion itself. The utopia is a strategic imagination providing motivation and justification for the quest and the conquest of the new world, rather than something which should be implemented.

Fyodorov's utopian project is vertical. This thoroughly changes the intuition about a "new world" which is to be constructed or colonized. It changes the key metaphors of the utopia as well as the character of the scientific coefficient which could be derived and elaborated from it. Human corporality becomes the central problem of the vertical utopia. Utopia is not an island overseas but cosmos itself. The means is not a ship but a spacecraft. The action is not a long voyage but an instant launch. We face no island populated by a society with rigid rules of life but a dynamic constellation of space aerostats, bases and stations controlled by the Space Center. In the vertical utopia, the visions for a tersely organized space-world and constitution of the human organism border on the idea of the abnormal in terms of the already established common sense for "natural life." The a prioiri forms of representation and perception of the natural life that ground the classical utopia are attacked radically.

The vertical utopian project marks the start of the colonization, that is, constructing of outer space. The horizontal geographical principle is ignored because the utopian space is not located overseas. It is not a particular locus but an intricate network-rootage of apparatuses and organs, a dynamic system of bases and transmissions, flying cities inhabited by "thinking reeds."

Vertical utopia mobilized science which invented aerostats and rockets, and turned metaphors and visions into reality. Outer space was discovered. Figurative revelation made possible the scientific discoveries. Precisely this visionary endeavor built the base and eventually prompted the conception of the Soviet outer-space doctrine.

It was Tsiolkovskii who turned vertical utopia into a science. His "free space" is an ingenious rationalization of Fyodorov's "common cause." Now the question stood as follows: How could humanity be launched into the "free space" of weightlessness? How could the body exist freely when weight-free? How will man's organism change in the conditions of "free space"? What jet-propelled prostheses will the freed body need in order to move and function in "free space"?

Vertical utopia goes further than horizontal utopia. It enacts a physically new space encompassing a morphologically new man whose socialization directly ensues from his reinvented nature. The first step of overcoming the earth forces was the erection of the body turning the animal into a human being. The next step is the parting of the body from the Earth. The body is to be ejected from Earth. The very act of ejection is presented as a sublime liturgical orgasm.

Summing up: we have four stages of the common cause—erection, orgasm, ejection of the very erected organ, spermatization of the outer space with new organisms. We are facing here the ultimate ejaculation where the erected organ itself is ejected once and forever. The gender of Earth is changed. It is no more the womb but rather a spermary. Earth is envisaged as a grand testicle of the dead fathers which excites, refuels and launches the living body of the sons forever away. A radical emasculation takes place and liquidates the gender structure of the body, turning it into an universal organ of human prosperity. Thus everlasting life is agitated. And *the wings of the soul will then become wings of the body.* The body takes off.

*I was driven towards lunacy.*
        *Tsiolkovskii*

BAKHTIN ORCHESTRATES

THE CHOIR OF THE SEXLESS VOICES

I find Bakhtin's enterprise with the dialogical principle absolutely sexless. He professes different forms of a gender-neutralized communal life.

1. Bakhtin directs the dialogue to the beyond-existence of a Super-addressee or an ultimate Paradigm which the dialogue always addresses and has it as its ultimate objective. The dialogue is an integrity of voices (polyphony), it is a resounding *harmonium* and *decorum* in a state of everlasting completion because the Super-addressee is never present in it. The Paradigm never descends completely into it.

Voices not bodies take part in the dialogue. The voice is a special vibration that immediately implements consciousness in a body. It is a Pegasus that ever gallops through the ongoing dialogue. The voice is a winged androgyne that transgresses the sex determination of the body into the sexless nature of the Angel. The voice is a consciousness projecting out of the body. It is a messenger who invades the dialogue. In the space of the dialogue we have only messengers of sex differences and corporal peculiarities but they themselves are sexless. Voices get amplified through the dialogue and it is precisely this sound image that the Super-addressee receives. The dialogue sounds, it does not show. The ostentatious principle of life is reduced in it. The dialogue abstracts consciousness from the bodies. And the Ideas depart from corpo-reality through *laughter.*

The dialogue speaks through us and not inversely for it was set prior to any utterance. The dialogue subdues the sex determination and brings people closer to the presence of the Super-addressee. The dialogue makes us "people of the moonlight"—if I may use Rosanov's metaphor for the sexless beings.

2. Bakhtin's vision of the carnival is congested with a brutal collective corpo-reality. The carnival, contrary to dialogue, maximizes the ostentatious element of life. Here we have only participation of bodies. The carnival surmounts the sex limitations through a drastic exchange of sex and class tokens that goes on in it: cross-dressing, symbolic trans- and-dis-gendering and other transmutations of the otherwise stable-featured social bodies. The carnival is an anatomical excess of ripped off and then not properly attached sex identifications.

The voices that take part in the dialogue originate in between the carnival bodies. And the dialogical principle subdues the *carnival laughter* in the sphere of the Super-addressee. Laughter swells into dialogue.

Through laughter the tokens of sexuality become utterly loose and detached from the bodies. Precisely the sex tokens are charged with the utter laughter and the sexual economy of laughter is the major one in the carnival. Laughter is the initial stage where a voice or a rhizome of voices emerges.

And Bakhtin sees in Dostoevskii's fiction precisely this ascending transformation from *carnival bodies* through *laughter* into independent *voices* crossing the primordial dialogue and the consequent formation of the *Ideas* that take off in order to address God with piety or profanation.

3. The strong voice induces an autonomous consciousness which Bakhtin considers ideologically enacted (e.g., Dostoevskii's character). The *idea-logos* is the sublime of the *dia-logos*. The ideologist is an individual with a body which is carnival proper (bearing the ambivalence of the collective elemental force) and a voice that abstracts from this body strategically oriented consciousness. Dostoevskii satisfies Bakhtin's vision of the universal order and the everlasting historical becoming of literature: a monstrous and criminal human interior turned inside out and shaken in laughter generates polyphony that is doomed to resound in the world and to transgress sex and gender by dropping out bodies and blowing out voices.

Voices arise and fall as Angels do.

## GASTEV: THE SOCIAL-ENGINEERING MACHINE

*There is a sense of fate about working in The Central Institute of Labor and this has made the possibility and the necessity of work wider even to the extent of working on the state apparatus.*

*I am deeply interested in two major ideas and I would like to convey their objective here as far as it is possible for me to do that. The first one I will call*
bio-energetics.

*The second one I will call*

organic-energetics.

*The first objective is to incite in the contemporary
man a special methodology towards a continuous biological improvement, towards biological ingenuity and
metamorphosis. The second objective is to come up with
a supreme organizational condensation, to come up
with methods for organizational switches along the
whole spectrum of life in its intricate and tremendous
complex.*

*In my life I had to be for long periods a revolution-
ary, a mechanic-constructor and an artist. And I came
to the conviction that the supreme expression in work,
which I believe was in everything that I did, was actually the*

engineering.

*The creative engineering applied to the organizational
work of construction as well as to the work of reconstruction of the human being is the very supreme scientific and artistic wisdom. The ultimate artistic wisdom
consists in the relentless work of the knife that*

classifies and analyses.

*And this is why for the present moment of construction
of The Central Institute of Labor I have to work with an
exceptional dedication and energy on the creation of the
so-called*

social-engineering machine

*which I recognize as the major thing we had to work on
during the decades of our artistic, organizational and
revolutionary activity. Just three words—*

pattern, directing and leader

*which theoretically express the general laws of kinetics,
and practically comprise the alphabet of each machine—
just these laws for me seem to open for the present moment a space of infinite horizons. And according to my
abilities I apply these laws not only to the creation of
specific organizational norms but also to draw some
conclusions for the retransforming and*

biological transformation

*of the modern man.*

*Gastev (1971, 15–16)*

Remember Gastev, that zealous poet of the Proletcult movement? His
vigorous verses are full of organic-mechanical imagery that merges
with the lava which erupts out of gigantic furnaces, melts and performs
stunning transfigurations. He professes a total political and biological

impact upon the world accomplished by the proletarian unified body that has been reinvented by materialistic science in special laboratories and has acquired a hitherto unseen omnipotent physical and mental constitution. A major dream and goal for the proletarian poets (those "engineers of the human psyche") was how to become engineers of the human body as well as to implant into its physique the "bold metaphors," to impregnate it with prodigious visions and thus to remake it. Implementation of the proletarian Word in proletarian Body—this was the final cause of the arts. Hence the works of Gastev have to be read as blueprints that project the formation of the future world and the man who inhabits it.

The poets-engineers knew clearly that the world they have invented is not designed for the humans presently dwelling on the earth. The new world is pernicious for them because they simply do not have the physical ability to face it and to sojourn in it. Only humans of a special make could live on the sun. The goal of the revolutionary arts was to design and to implement precisely this new special make of the proletarian body. Soon after that Stalin (the name implies steel), standing in front of Lenin's Mummy, uttered the words: "We, the communists, are people of a special make. We are made of a special material."

## Labor as Implementation of Social Engineering

*Our path leads through the poetry of machines, from the*
*bungling citizen to the perfect electric man.*
*    The new man, free of unwieldiness and clumsiness,*
*will have the light, precise movements of machines.*
Dziga Vertov (1984, 8)

A campaign of mass social engineering took place. Through labor, the bodies were remade in the factories. Through labor, bodies were corrected in the camps. Camps and factories were the grand laboratories for reinventing the human physique. They mass-produced the compact proletarian body as the inhabitant of communism. For communism turned out to be a world that requires special instruction, abilities and skills for one to live in it.

## Party Use and Abuse of Social Engineering

A correction was made with historical consequences that we must be aware of—at a certain point the political purposes of proletarian art were reformulated as Party ones, the Proletcult was abolished by Lenin, modernism was implemented in the Party program and power techniques, and thus terminated. The world-building metaphors and visions of modernism were translated in the terms of power-building that became a total concern of the Party. And Party power became the only social engineer who was remaking and reinventing its own population for almost a century.

The definition of the social engineering was: Party itself creates the people it stands for. Party power, following a certain Idea, designs its own social basis and constituency. It disciplines the historical subject summoned to fulfill the Party project.

Through usurping power the Red Party comes out of its underground stage with a clear-cut plan how to proceed further and to build up its own ideology. The Party has to provide itself with constituency holding the majority in the society and disciplined automatically to build up the future. The large-scale industrialization was a political action with only one goal—to produce the Party constituency. Labor was designed to (re)produce the working-class body as the social basis of the Party. Thus Party power provided itself with historical representatives.

RESTARTING THE GLOBE

**OR HOW PLATONOV FIGURES THE END**

## The Cosmic Anarchy

*Ah-ah-ah, ha-ha, ho-ho!*
*Laughter and Love, copulating with Melancholy*
*and Hate, pressed together in the mighty, convulsive*
*passion of bestial lust. Long live the psychology of*
*contrasts! . . .*
*Wait! Melancholy! Black yawning ulcers of agony*
*cover the pale, terror-stricken face of heaven. The earth*
*trembles with fear beneath the mighty wrathful blows of*
*its Children! Oh, you cursed, loathsome things! They*
*tear at its fair, tender flesh and bury their withered,*
*starving melancholy in the flowing blood and fresh*
*wounds of its body. The world is dying! Ah! Ah! Ah!*
*cry millions of tocsins. Ah! Ah! Ah! roar the giant can-*
*non of alarm. Destruction! Chaos! Melancholy! The*
*world is dying!*
*Such is the poetry of our melancholy! Death to the*
*world Civilization!*

*Anarcho-Futurist Manifesto, 1919*
*(Avrich 1973, 53–54)*

The reading of Platonov I will embark on, considers the ideas of Russian anarchism as crucial for a thorough understanding of his shocking works. Platonov is an author of the total vision. Platonov is not a critic of a forthcoming system as the literary criticism has it. He is not an anti-utopianist either who shows the dark side, the annihilating force, the verso of the revolution. He criticizes nothing, he analyses nothing. He does not belong to any rationalistic, analytical or critical tradition and he does not make use of them. Considered from such a perspective, his vision seems to be either rather naive or sick, but not distant and alienated from the stunning pictures it conjures up. His entire being is passionately involved rather then detached from the monstrous reality emerging through his fiction. His vision demolishes the old impaired world and nourishes on its rotting matter and gangrene. He exhausts through his imagination the total collapse and decline of the old world. Even the corporal element of the revolution bears the virus and is struck by the same sickness unto death that ruins the old world. The body of the revolution is a scapegoat that has to be dismembered, torn apart, decomposed and turned into a nutritious mud for the future creation. After the grand performance, the entire corpo-reality of the revolution is to be drained into the nutritious slops and a new body has to emerge out of them.

There is no critique. There works an ecstatic vision for the universal orgy of revolution that periodically is overcome with melancholy and grief but soon bursts out again vehemently. Platonov's protagonist has an impaired body and psyche and being aware of his destiny he advances to the very end of the total submergence in the global mud and dreams new formation. Black and Red—these are the symbols of the world anarchy and the banner of anarchism is made out of them. The positive and the negative principles work together as an ensemble. Black fits the revolutionary body. Red fits the revolutionary idea. The body will die. The idea will survive.

The anarchist movement played a prominent role in the Russian Revolution. Later it was liquidated by the one-party politics of Lenin. That was because the anarchists fought (by definition) against the state and any centralized institution as a form of social government. The most alarming phenomenon for them was the establishment of the Soviet centralized state system ruled by a single personal will to power and congested by a huge inert and rigid Party majority which gradually strangled the revolution.

Anarchism is a total strategy conducting the final obliteration of all limitations and differences in the world. It professes a natural stateless condition of society. The anarchists' credo—to regain the original Paradise of human life before the Fall and prior to any crime-guilt-punishment complex, prior to any kind of repression; to get rid of any kind of supervision and authority. Society is a single organism and every part contributes equally to its completeness and accomplishments. Any institutionalization of life impairs this organism. Any official hierarchy mutilates it.

Anarchism, as Mannheim points out in his *Ideology and Utopia,* is an orgiastic vision of life that raves of salvation and liberation. Anarchism aims at a restitution of the initial ecstasy of life where desires get completely exhausted through communal jubilation and manifestation and nothing remains to be secondarily discharged though violation of the natural order.

Anarchistic vision is ecstatic, orgiastic, excessive and equally melancholic, mournful and funereal. Anarchist economy of life leads to an acute excitement and then sudden exhaustion of corporality. The body is groggy between shocks and melancholy. Anarchy is a fusion of Red and Black.

Platonov figures a cosmic anarchy in his fiction. Anarchism is the principle of his visionary world.

## The Foundation Pit(fall)   A Platonov Novel

*What are you building?—I want to dig a subterranean*
*passage. Some progress must be made. My station up*
*there is much too high  We are digging the pit of Babel.*
                    *Kafka,* Parables and Paradoxes


### The Earth as Double Metaphor: Planet and Globe

*After all, the whole earthly sphere, all its softness, will*
*soon be taken in precise, iron hands.*
            *Platonov,* The Foundation Pit *(1973, 84)*

The figure of the *planet* Earth plays a crucial role in the legacy of the Russian political art of the 1920s and the rhetoric of the Proletcult. It expresses two strategic ideas—that the proletarian revolution as an unique and ultimately radical action has planetary significance because it affects the totality of the planet, its entire territory, its physical and social nature, its biopolitical constitution. And second—the Revolution is proved, justified, regulated and supervised precisely by a science known as *dialectical materialism.* This science elaborates an all-embracing and unprecedented biopolitical-engineering plan for re building the entirety of the world and reinventing human nature. Science of that kind induces the idea of the Earth as a grand laboratory organized in outer space and making the human being capable of intervening in the progress of the universe.

For that purpose the proletarian body is to acquire a new hyper-corporal constitution in order to become the governor of the universe. The Earth must not be any more an immense inert lump revolving in the universe. The Earth is now the original *perpetum mobile* made use of by the Revolution as the ultimate vehicle for travelling through outer space and reassembling it.

The Earth represented as *globe* (not as *planet*) induces a different intuition. The globe is a miniature, a model, a geopolitical mapping, blueprint and plan of the planet itself. The globe represents the Earth as an object observed and supervised as if from outer space. And the proletarian mind casts on the globe its stern gaze, a gaze which cuts out the political face of the planet. A tough worker stretches out his iron hand to speed up the spinning of the globe and thus accelerates the progress.

The Earth figured as a *vehicle, object* and *instrument* of the ongoing Revolution cooperates with the radical idea from the turn of the century for an expansion in outer space, a geopolitical "cutting and pasting" of boundaries and countries. The same idea enacted a fundamental social engineering aimed at inventing and testing the new human creature who was to operate with the Machine-Earth. A human being of a special make was professed to run the campaign for the conquest of the universe. This same being was supposed to conduct the Earth through space, constantly improving the performance of the jet-propelled engine assembled into it.

The *globe* implies geopolitical planning. The *planet* is the ultimate spacecraft. The Earth is an *arena* that stages Revolution. These three icons appear constantly in the proletarian arts and letters of the 1920s. We can observe the expansion of Earth imagery in the verses of the Proletcult, of futurism, the Left's expressionism, and in the assemblages of constructivism, in Maiakovskii's play *Misteria Buff,* and so on. The Earth is a grand work of proletarian arts and sciences performing revolution.

Influenced directly by Gastev and his ferro-concrete verses that cut through and plow the ground of poetry, Platonov glorifies the Earth as a machine of a special construction. He demonstrates in his prose the grand political commitment of the Earth and its specific service to the revolution.

The Earth is the vehicle proper of the universal revolution. That is why it needs scientific monitoring and control accompanied with periodical testing, repair and adjustment. The Earth as a machine—this is the issue of Platonov's article entitled "Repair of the Earth."

In *The Foundation Pit* the monstrous body of the Earth is experienced as a mythic creature which obeys only to its own special metabolism, effective systems of digestion, secretion and sanitation. The human beings cut the skin of the Earth with spades and iron wedges and thus try to get connected with the internal circulation of the earth's organism. The new beings refuse to live among the ruins of history any more, among those blisters and dead tissues stuck on the skin of the Earth. They have to contact the life systems of the cosmic monster after they break through its dead scales formed in the period of the bourgeois culture.

The circuit of an everlasting life is set when the iron proletarian blade contacts the warm ground. And the proletarians of the *Pit* plug the spades in the soft orifice of the monster-earth and thus penetrate and excite it to the quick.

Stab Earth with spade!

*Having said this Chiklin shoved his spade down into*
*the top soft layer of the earth concentrating downwards*
*his apathetic-thoughtful face. Voshchev also began to*
*burrow deep into the soil, letting all his strength into*
*the spade.*

The Foundation Pit, 21

The Iron was proclaimed the revolutionary counterpart of the Ground element. The spectacular conjugation of those two strategic substantives is the major poetic operation in the proletarian arts. Revolution provides the poet with iron feather and language with humus-like structure—the soil and the plow, and thus fertilizes life.

## Revolutionary Substances and Substantives

*Earth* is the primal substantive in the revolutionary grammar and *soil* is the primal revolutionary substance in the list of elements, materials and fabrics of reality which one can extract from *The Foundation Pit*. We face various descriptions of formation and transformation of the substances on/in the Earth and thus we can observe a goal-oriented conversion of the material forms of life. The ground itself is charged with revolution, which is made obvious through its sudden transformations and substantial mutation. The Earth performs stunning transfigurations and thus stages on its surface the excessive work of the Revolution.

Platonov shows the Revolution as an event utterly experienced throughout the infinite material element of life, throughout its immeasurable diversity of liquid and solid, alive and dead substances which rot away or propagate because of lusty or lethal forces hidden in them. In Platonov's work the course of Revolution can be traced through the constant changes in earthly matter. The progress of Revolution in life is performed as a spectacular bacchanalia and intoxication of the earthly substances.

The Earth exposes dazzling evidences, profane and drastic pictures testifying to the grand transfiguration of the face of the world handled by the revolutionary artistic mind. This is because the class interest runs even through the natural circuits of Earth. The ground becomes the main conductive element of the advancing proletarian interest and will to power.

The decomposed matter left on the battlefields becomes a powerful fertilizer for the new shoots to appear on the stem of Revolution. And the stench released stimulates the work of mind.

### Plot and Scenes

*Only now did he see the center of the city with devices in the process of assembling in it. . . . Separately from nature, in the bright spot of electricity, people labored eagerly, raising up brick walls, marching with burdens of freight along the plank nightmare of the scaffoldings. Voshchev contemplated for a long time the construction of a tower unfamiliar to him.*

The Foundation Pit, *12*

In the novel we have two main scenes of the action—a foundation pit is being dug at the outskirts of a small town to open the place for the erection of a communal proletarian home; then a huge raft is nailed together in a collective farmyard by means of which the proletarians ship the kulaks away on the ocean far from the sight of the working class. The protagonists move from the first place to the second, one dragging along a chain of tied-together coffins. After fulfilling their work on the raft they get back to the pit.

It is indicated in a sentence that in the center of the small town a tower is being constructed but the narrative never comes back to that place.

A scene of a dying woman in a deserted factory symbolizes the final coalescence of rotting flesh, soil and collapsing construction.

*The factory had now become lower for it had gradually grown into the ground, and its yard was deserted.*

The Foundation Pit, *58*

### The New Ark

*What coffins?*
*The enormous naked man swollen from wind and anguish did not say his word immediately, at first he*

*dropped his hat and strained himself to figure out . . .*
*perhaps he was exhausted, or perhaps he was dying off*
*by small parts in the course of life.*

    *Coffins!—he reported in a hot, wooly voice—We*
*stored up board coffins in the cave, and you are digging*
*up the whole gully. Give the coffins back!*

    *Chiklin said that yesterday evening one hundred*
*empty coffins had really been discovered near the north*
*picket; two of them he had appropriated for the little*
*girl—in one he had made up her bed for the future . . .*
*and the other he had given her as a gift for her toys and*
*a kind of child's household: let her have her own Red*
*Agit-Corner.*

                            The Foundation Pit, *73*

It happens that after some toil and tough work in the pit the protagonists leave behind the spades because they have to drag up
chained-together coffins to a collective farm where they start assembling the raft.

To sum up—a communal pit is being dug, coffins are being
dragged, one of them is arranged to become the Red entertaining
room for a dying girl, a raft is made for social sanitation purposes.
An enormous amount of junk and drains, of useless objects and remains is being accumulated on the face of the Earth turning it into
a morgue.

And the Earth, keeping the apathetic manners of a snake, victori-
ously swallows up things scattered over its surface. The last shelters (before the ground finally takes over life) are the pit, and the coffins, and
the wooden barracks where the grave-diggers of capitalism dwell.
These are the revolutionary replicas of Noah's Ark.

If the hero digs deeper and deeper it gets warmer and warmer
because the Earth interior opens its soft lubricated uterine depth.
One can say that parallel to the digging, the symbols of Life sink
deep into the Earth. And above the ground the symbols of Death
spread out.

The Earth gets as cold as a grenade lobbed into a chilly night, a moment before it blows up.

*He began to dig in the ground, but the ground had*
*already frozen, and Chiklin had to cut the earth into*
*chunks and to pry it out in whole dead pieces. Deeper*
*down things went softer and warmer; Chiklin drove*
*into it with cutting blows of his iron spade and soon*
*was concealed into the silence of the earth's interior.*

                            The Foundation Pit, *154*

## Dejection

*Without truth, my body grows weak, and I cannot keep*
*myself nourished on labor. During the process of pro-*
*duction I became contemplative and I was dismissed.*
The Foundation Pit, 15

Throughout the novel the proletarian psyche suffers an acute dejection accompanied by a dejection of the bodies on the earth's surface. Thus the homogeneous alloy of the revolutionary dejection of mind and body is synthesized. The mournful physiognomy of the Earth's matter and the melancholic meditation overwhelming the proletarian consciousness mark the first, the negative phase of the communist transfiguration of life.

*From around the village he had gathered all of the*
*wretched and rejected objects, all the loss and all the*
*junk of oblivion, for the sake of socialist retribution. . . .*
*Voshchev, without completely realizing, had thrifty ac-*
*cumulated in his bag the material remains of lost people,*
*who like him had lived without truth and who had come*
*to their end before the victorious end.*
The Foundation Pit, 131

The protagonist takes on the mission of the exorcist who in clear consciousness and self-awareness has to trap in his body the universal deformity and monstrosity of life, has to evoke the universal void and vanity in his soul in order to end them there. Thus the very body and psyche of the hero become the point of mental devastation and physical termination of the human being, of this imperfect and cursed creature doing wrong on the Earth.

*Having liquidated the kulaks . . . Zhachev did not relax,*
*he became even more nervous without being clear why . . .*
*boredom and mourning arise within his breast. After*
*all, the stratum of the mournful monstrosities was not*
*needed in socialism and they will soon liquidate him too*
*in the distant quiet.*
The Foundation Pit, 125

## The Earth as Lethal Chamber

*He smiled enthusiastically, and gave orders to those*
*surrounding him to mobilize the collective farm for a fu-*
*neral procession so that all the people should feel the*

*majesty of death during the time of the progressing*
*bright moment of socialization of private property.*
The Foundation Pit, 90

Along with the grand construction campaign and class-justified purge of humankind demonstrated in the novel, certain lethal processes are in progress on the surface of the Earth involving the whole diversity of objects, bodies and vermin. I made a list of the most demonstrative phenomena taking place in the *The Foundation Pit* and testifying to the methodical and apathetic setting in of universal death, creating a hitherto unseen funereal appearance of the Earth.

These are the signs of the negative stage:

—a relentless march of death
—the weakness in the bodies grows
—it is getting colder and colder on the Earth's surface
—the monstrosity of the people is growing
—the void expands
—people suffer lack of truth and meaning of life
—the proletarian psyche is overwhelmed by a swelling anxiety
   and anguish
—the ideology of life vanishes
—the meditative mind of the protagonist gradually degenerates
   into a stare cutting through the void
—things available above the ground sink irreversibly into it
—the growing apathy of the characters often is violated by unmotivated bursts of exaltation and outrage which are exhausted
   through a zealous digging down into the Earth
—life processes gradually slow down to the rhythm of a funereal
   procession
—a suggestive mourning and omnipresent vanity set in on the
   Earth
—life ceremoniously passes into a state of coma
—the Being sinks into the deep embrace of death

Proletarian Mind submerges into mourning and melancholy.

## The Genesis Restarted

*I am sure the advent of the proletarian art will take an*
*indecent form. We grow from the earth and all its filth;*
*and all that is in earth is in us too.*

*Don't be afraid, we will purge ourselves; we abhor*
*our deformity, we are going out of the mud vigorously.*

> *This is our commitment. The soul of the world will*
> *grow out of our deformity.*
> *Platonov (1989, 38–39)*

The Genesis is to be restarted.

There are two things that could help proletarians to start the human world again—the first is the *perpetum mobile* of the Earth itself. The second one is the *materialistic science* that has reached the sublime stage of proletarian self-consciousness and thus has become capable of handling any process of Earth. It is precisely the scientific mind of the revolution that will restart the world and reshape human creature out of a new humus.

Before the second molding takes place, proletarians have to suffer the negative stage of world anarchy, the stage of being fused together in one substantial element. The second formation needs the universal substance and that divine primordial mud has to be resynthesized.

For the time being, proletarians have to install the equipment for the genesis, to lay down their own bodies as material for this generic operation and to turn the mechanism on. Thus the double revolutionary commitment of the proletarian consciousness and of the proletarian body is finally fulfilled.

The laborer's hand has to put together a grand electrical installation (electricity disseminates revolution) and to restart the chain reaction of the genesis. The materialistic mind will conduct the process, preventing any breakdown of the circuit. And they, the former humans, have to purge out their diversity and difference, their existential disability of being separate bodies. Their bodies, which suffer gender determination, are doomed to copulate in order to reach some imperfect unity and thus to propagate and engender the same corporal diversity further and further again without knowing any conciliation.

Without doubt proletarians are born longing for an integrated communal body. And the womb of the Earth will deliver this futuristic body in cooperation with the proletarian mind—the obstetrician.

> *The uterine excavation for the communal house of the*
> *future life was ready; now the cornerstone was to be laid*
> *into it.*
> The Foundation Pit, *80*

The Earth is a miraculous jet-propelled womb flying through space, a stunning catapult launching the new Adam into the universe.

Now, as Gastev preaches, they have to compose a proletarian collective, an impersonal and anonymous body which makes it possible for any part of it to be considered a link in a chain reaction.

Let this laboring Anonym plunge into the soft depth of the Earth and get dissolved into it, thus restarting the Genesis.

*He laid down on the table between the corpses and per-
sonally died.*
>                                         The Foundation Pit, *90*


## An Integrated Social Body

*Voshchev was given a spade, he gripped it with his
hands, he was just about to mine the truth out of the
earthly dust; homeless Voshchev was agreeable not to
possess sense of existence but wished at least to contemplate it in the corporal substance of his neighbor.*
>                                 The Foundation Pit, *19–20*

And Platonov's characters keep digging the pit and suffering progressive exhaustion and weakness, and get more and more deformed but penetrate the Earth deeper and deeper and thus open the chasm where their separate and monstrous bodies will sink together into the soft abyss, from which their integrated body will be later delivered.

Before this happens, they have to excommunicate the alien corpus of the kulaks built out of hostile and pernicious class substances. That is precisely what the proletarians do in the novel—they assemble a raft and purge the kulaks away in the waters of the ocean. The liquid (water) here is recognized as a purging substance which drains the rejected and excommunicated by the revolution, washing away foul reality, materials and residues. When the genesis starts again the total liquid mass will evaporate into nothingness.

The proletarian body communicates with the Earth (not with the water), that is, with solid matter. Thus it can get consolidated into one homogenous block.

## End of the Negative Stage

The digging of a foundation pit and the draining of the bodies not evoked to dwell in it—this is the first, the negative stage of the revolution, when every separate body dies on the earth and surrenders to the Earth. Earth dissolves and absorbs the prodigious amount of junk scattered on it, digests the ruins of history and thus the metabolism of genesis is sustained. But the point is that precisely thus the Earth decomposes and erases all the signs, marks, traces and tokens of the past.

The bad class substance (bourgeois) is excommunicated through water and the good class substance (proletarian), together with the whole substantial memory of humankind, melt together in the Earth. All objects inducing recollection of history, all ruins of the past, museum collections of the old world, its remains and heaped junk gradually sink into the earth by loosing identity and merging their outlines. Any past and any memory that bears evidences is dissolved into the omnipresent oblivion brought by the negative stage. Thus the old world is finally abolished.

The *apocalypsis transfiguris* of the Earth has two stages and the novel here discussed depicts the first one—for before erecting they have to dig, for to prepare the substance of the future integrated body they have to fuse together their own bodies, for before the corporality gains back the truth of life they have to suffer the void lack of sense and ideology.

*Without ideology Voshchev also had physically weak-*
*ened to such a degree that he could not lift his ax, and*
*he lay there in the snow; no matter what, there was no*
*truth in the world, or, perhaps, it had existed within*
*some plant or in some heroic vermin, but some wander-*
*ing wretch had come by and eaten up the plant or tram-*
*pled on the vermin below, and had then died himself in*
*an autumn ravine, and his body was blown into noth-*
*ingness by the wind.*
The Foundation Pit, 112

Evaporated tears return as divine rain.

*Voshchev, leaning back against the coffin, looked up*
*from the cart to the dead mass mist of the Milky Way.*
*He was waiting for the day when up there a resolution*
*will be promulgated on the termination of the eternity of*
*time, on atonement for the weariness of life.*
The Foundation Pit, 82

## The Universal Sex: Adam Disgendered

*Having found the Good in the sexual feeling, people*
*were petrified.*
Platonov (Vasil'ev 1982, 39)

An extreme concept of Proletcult ideology is that the power of class "consciousness will defeat and abolish sex and will become the center of humanity" (ibid). Class determination of life will abolish the sex differences in communism. For that purpose we must keep our communist awareness alert and this will close gradually the gender gap between man and woman.

Platonov insists on *virility* as the major feature of the future disgendered being. Woman according to him creates the gender difference.

Man is genderless by his origin—Adam before the Eve. He describes in the *Foundation Pit* a female pioneer detachment marching and advancing against the void. It is an orchestra of young girls with expressly virile bodies. These girls will survive the turbulence of the revolution because of the growing virility in their bodies.

The new man has to acquire the virile physique of Adam. This makes Platonov argue that the human creature of the future will obtain and maximize masculine body constitution. The feminine body will vanish either through a progressing virilization or through death. In the novel we have two conditions of the female body, either it gets virile and survives or it gets sick and finally faces death.

Femininity is the human sickness unto death.

What happens to the female beings in the novel, excluding the virile girls just mentioned, is demonstratively clear. We encounter the striking picture of a dying woman in a deserted factory which gradually sinks into the ground. Her daughter sleeps on the mother's stomach. Then comes the protagonist and takes the girl away from the already dead mother. But it turns out that the girl is struck by a bad disease. She is doomed to die because of existential lack of virility in her body. Without getting virile the female body gets deadly sick. And the novel ends with the death of the girl. The decline of the youth in *The Foundation Pit* represented by the sick girl, is caused by her fatal disadvantage of being a completely female creature.

*Let the various dead objects keep her. The dead bodies*
*are as plenty as the alive ones and they are not bored*
*among each other.*
The Foundation Pit, 67

Femininity withers away. It has to be regarded as an initial impairment of the human being that the social engineering of the Revolution will repair.

*As a deformity I can only hail your opinion.*
The Foundation Pit, 71

## *A Surge of Protoplasm Obliterates Diversity*

*Communism is a society mostly for males.*
Platonov (Vasil'ev 1982, 39)

Here the old myth of Genesis works but slightly corrected. According to the legend the woman was made out of a part of the male body. Precisely thus man lost his corporal completeness and became deformed because of this. The female sex turns to be an even greater deformation being a part ripped off Man which grew up into a completely different creature, into an ultimately manifested partiality. Before restarting the genesis, proletarians need the occurrence of a retrieving process, that is, the transgendering of woman into man. Then follows the retrieval of the primordial human substance by transforming the communal flesh into mud (the proto-plasma). The final act is the formation of Adam's body anew but without any violation of its original completeness, of His corporal unity.

Going further one can predict the second, the positive stage of the revolutionary liturgy envisaged by Platonov—human beings merge together into One single body (organism) which dwells and acts on the Earth without facing any *other* to fight with. Vision of that kind demonstrates a revolutionary perspective far beyond the common idea of collectivization and condensing proletariat in one communal place. Not just a working-class assembly-life and communal corporality but the unique Adam is the body dreamt of here.

**ARCHITECTURAL TROPE:**

**MANDELSTAM AND MELNIKOV**

Fight the Void!

In this section I shall be dealing with two major ideas of modern architecture as an art that can build a perfect and prosperous communal life. The divine vocation of architecture is to design the pattern and the tools for mankind to structure a space of salvation. Moreover, architecture is the only art that gives an unique opportunity for the master to settle down in the space of his masterpiece and the creator to find peace in the interiors of his creation. The visionary sojourns in the interior of the vision.

We shall approach two opposite visions of architecture as developed in the works of Mandelstam, written before the Revolution, and in the projects of the professional architect Melnikov, made immediately after the Revolution. Both artists profess architecture as sublime realm where art immediately builds eternal life. Architecture can resolve the original problems of being and save the errant souls roaming around this doomed world. Both men see the ultimate objective of architecture in providing the sublime environment for the universal union of people. Architecture is the capital art that through its structures surpasses the limits of natural human body and thus utterly unfolds it in the space. Architecture carries the human physique beyond its material limits and endows it with tremendous magnitude.

Mandelstam sees an exalting human physiology enacted in the masterpieces of the medieval architecture (prerevolutionary vision), while Melnikov designs an architecture of anesthesia for the future inhabitants of communism (post revolutionary vision). As ever the ultimate visions emerge from the grand figures; Adam and the Crucified.

## The Original Story

The Lord made the world and the creatures, in the beginning.

Then He formed the Man from dust and called upon him to give names to all the livestock. And Adam announced the names. Then the Lord fashioned the Woman from a rib taken out of Man's rib-cage.

After Adam names the creatures that the Lord had created, he committed sin. Eve beguiled Adam. He tasted the forbidden fruit of knowledge and his eyes opened. Adam saw Eve naked, and he desired her, and he knew her.

Man realized his body was naked, after the Fall. Nakedness replaced Blindness. Sin summoned sight. Thus Man saw the creatures, named in blindness and ignorance, naked.

Nakedness exposes bodies who bear names.

On the same day Adam was dropped on Earth. And Earth attracted him with its elemental force. Gravitation made his body ponderous. Thus, dragging no fetters he was captivated for life. On Earth bodies bear names and are stigmatized to be naked. Adam was interned in nakedness. Thus punishment took place.

Naked, Adam rushed in panic to hide in his own shadow. And he started to build up space, to load it with allegorical devices, to structure it. He launched a grand construction campaign. He composed the grand Book of Life. Thus Adam saves the people.

The space grows because man survives.

## Adamism

*The new Adam came not on the sixth day of Creation
in a virgin and intact world, but in Russia's modern
times. He looked around with this clear and penetrating
eye of his . . . and his affectionate vision embraced all
and everything.*

                    *S. Gorodetskii (Trifonov 1987, 472)*

Different poetic groups of the modernist movement and especially the acmeists to whom Mandelstam belongs, were preoccupied with the image and virile physique of Adam—the progenitor, the first man, the name-giver who uttered the proper names of things, who committed the original sin, who perceived nudity emerging through his errant vision.

The new verse has the assignment to resurrect the original condition of the Word. Poetic creation, according to acmeists is a resurrection of Adam's proper word. The word of the progenitor is always identified with his body. Precisely as words do, the bodies of predecessors descend down through history and time reaching the actual humans. Resurrection of the original speech means resurrection of the body that pronounces it. The recurrence of the beginning through poesis is termed the *acme* of creation and contemplation.

Rozanov, who advances a sexual doctrine that goes against orthodox Christian teachings, also preaches about the advent of the original, the innocent, the sexually ignorant Adam:

> . . . about the man existing before any sex, mastering a body which precedes any gender and rejoicing his "moonlight" personality.
>
> Adam from whom Eve has not yet emerged—the first and complete Adam. He is older then the "first man who began to reproduce." He looks at the world with an older eye; he has in his nature older tales, older songs of the earth. In the cosmological and religious sequence, he precedes reproduction. Reproduction came later, it came later and covered him over, just as the present-day layers of the earth have covered over the Devonian or Jurassic formations. He is the Devonian formation, reproduction is that of the present day. (1978, 132)

## Mandelstam: Physiology of the Stone

*To build means to fight the void, to hypnotize space. The
fine arrow of the Gothic bell-tower is wicked for its
whole idea is to stab the sky for being void.
We imply the particularity of man that makes him
special, in a much more significant notion of organism.
Acmeists share their love for organism and organization
with the physiological genius of the Middle Ages. . . .
That which in the thirteen century seemed a logical development of the notion of organism—the Gothic cathedral—now produces the aesthetic effect of monstrosity.
Notre Dame is a feast of physiology, its Dionisyan orgy.
We do not want to entertain ourselves by walking
around the "forest of symbols" because we possess the
virgin, slumberous forest of a divine physiology, the infinite complexity of our dark organism.*
                    *Mandelstam,* The Morning of Acmeism

In 1913 Mandelstam published a collection of poems called *Stone* (*Kamen'*). The same year he wrote one of the major manifestos of acmeism called *The Morning of Acmeism* published later in 1919. In these two works

Mandelstam professes the new metaphysical and poetic values of acmeism harking back to the Middle Ages and brooding on the ingenious influence of physiology on architecture as expressed in the formidable bodies of the cathedrals which bear the major corporal code of those great times. He extols the stone as the most real (solid) material of creation ever found on earth. Man was made out of dust but he himself creates divine monuments and sanctuaries out of the most consolidated matter—stone. In the stone flesh is overcome. The figure of the cathedral represents an exalted human physiology turned into enormous work that accommodates in its profound interior the corpus of the entire congregation.

It is a *locus communis* that the cathedral body figuratively represents the body of Christ—the ultimate man—and thus symbolically unites the worshippers. The sacred structure is a petrified (stone) figure of man and manifests his maximized physique. In the verse collection mentioned above, there is a poem called "Notre Dame" that completely demonstrates the vision for a secret identity between physiology and architecture that a new poetry has to pursue and a new life has to realize.

## The Vault Where Genders Merge

Notre Dame

Где римский судия судил чужой народ—
Стоит базилика, и радостный и первый,
Как некогда Адам, распластывая нервы,
Играет мышцами крестовый легкий свод.

Но выдает себя снаружи тайный план—
Здесь позаботиласъ подпружных арок сила
Чтоб масса грузная стены не сокрушила
И свода дерзкого бездействует таран.

Стихийный лабиринт, непостижимый лес,
Души готической рассудочная пропасть,
Египетская мощь и христианства робость,
С тростинкой рядом—дуб, и всюду царь—
    отвес.

Но чем виматедьней, твердыня Notre
    Dame,
Я изучал твои чудовищные ребра,
Тем чаще думал Я:из тяжести недоброй
И я когда-нибудь прекрасное создам.

NOTRE DAME  (a literal translation)

There where Roman judge judged an alien
    people
Stands a basilica and joyful and first,
As Adam once was, spreading out the
    nerves,
Plays with muscles the light rib vault.

But the secret plan reveals itself from with-
    out—
Here the strength of the flying buttresses has
    taken care.
That the ponderous mass not crush the wall,
And the battering ram of the bold vault is
    idle.

Elemental labyrinth, unfathomable forest,
The rational abyss of the Gothic soul,
Egyptian might and Christian modesty
Next to rood   an oak, everywhere plumb
    (the vertical) is the king

But the more attentively, O fortress Notre
    Dame,
I studied thy monstrous ribs,
The more often I thought: from a wild weight
Me too some time, I will create the beautiful.

1. *Adam as Virgin Dame.* Throughout the poem a graphic identification of *Adam* as *Notre Dame* is manifested. The structure of "Notre Dame" suggests a figure of Adam's virile body. The first stanza extols the joyful play of the male, still virgin physique. It emerges through the female figure of the cathedral which modifies its appearance into a mytho-genious Androgyne. Bisexual Eros rehabilitates as virgin Androgyne.

2. It is *the principal of equilibrium* that builds up the entire poem. A parity is established between the a priori opposed forces: masculinity/femininity; lightness/heaviness; the horizontal/vertical traction of the material. Transept and nave fit together into a Cross; a poetic equation appears between masses of people and ponderous masses of inert material; and so on.

The boss of the rib vault locks the mistic equilibrium that keeps the integrity of the elements in the structure. The key ornament keeps the cathedral Figure erect in Heavens and neutralizes the lethal gravitation (attraction) of Earth. The silhouette of the Crucifixion appears in every joint and prevents the collapse of the structure.

*Rib and groin.* These are major metaphors built in the poem that recall the creation of Man. They recall also the stabbed chest of the Crucified. The ascetic figure of Christ desecrated and suspended from the Cross gives the sacred pattern of the Christian construction of the world. The Cross sustains the ponderous mass of dead corpo-reality lest it fall down on the congregation flocked around it. There is a sublime scene of *The Pieta*—the lifeless body of the Crucified taken off the cross lying in the arms of the Virgin. *The Pieta* is the prototype of the Christian temple, where the lofty mien of the Virgin completes the vertical line and embraces the maltreated body of Christ, which completes the horizontal line of the temple. Notre Dame repeats this sacral composition.

The rib is a miraculous bone that shapes the physiology of breathing. Out of it a Master made a woman, formed the vault of a temple, honed a sword, bent a bow, erected the fortifications of Notre Dame. The cathedral resembles a gigantic ribcage which performs the respiration of the Holy Spirit descending on earth. It is suggestive that the metaphor of breathing proliferates throughout the entire collection *Stone*. It opens with a poem called "Breathing," which becomes a recurring poetic figure in the verses that follow. The torso of the cathedral implies a petrified breathing. The structure suggests a formidable ribcage that breathes.

3. The athletic physique of Adam emerges from the feminine torso of the cathedral and the name *Adam* rhymes with the name *Notre Dame*

in Russian. There is a constructive *coordination of gender symbols* which build up the archite(x)ture of the poem; phallic or uterine—battering ram and labyrinth, reed and oak, projection and cavity, unconquerable dark forest (Virgin) and the joyful, muscular torso (Adam).

4. *Sobornost'*. This is a key word in Russian Orthodox doctrine, as well as in Russian philosophical messianism, mysticism and moral codes of communal life. *Sobor* means cathedral, that is, a place where people gather to attain a transcendental mode of existence, their godlike unity and bliss. *Sobor* is a noun that comes from a verb that means to-gather (*sobirat'*) and *sobornost'* could be translated as people's togetherness in a congregational sense. People flock in the cathedral to absolve their sins and to dissolve the passion of their partial corporality through the immaculate communal body. The divine vocation of the Russian Messiah—be he a patron, a master or an artist—is to make people flock around his body and word, to make them merge in one collective body, and thus to save them. *Sobornost'* is elevated through different collectivist ideologies and doctrines into the most genuine principle of Russian common cause—the essence of Russiandom.

The poet rhymes *people* with the cruciform vault. The integrity of the rib vault sustains the cathedral torso like the crucifixion locks the sacred code of the congregation and keeps the integrity of its body.

Synonymy between the building metaphors is established: *sobor* + *svod* + *narod* = *sobornost* (cathedral + vault + people = togetherness). Here is another one: *cross* + *battering ram* + *vault* + *rib*. These are phallic figures of a tamed erection (Adam's rib-phallus bent as vault). Abundance of phallic tools and parts of the cathedral are wedged up in its uterine interior to support its ponderous masses. The whole structure stands as a gigantic petrified womb that looms in eternity. Here comes the *sobornost* principle—people get consolidated into one block-body. The stone cathedral by its solidified embrace grants people solidarity.

## Melnikov: Architecture of An Eternal Tranquility

*It is not by accident that in Fydorov's work the concept*
*of the tamale appears as the greatest achievement of hu-*
*man art. . . . It is the architectural ensemble that orga-*
*nizes the dead and heavy material masses according to*
*the laws of reason, beauty and harmony. Architecture,*
*this wonderful suspended fall, appears to Fyodorov*
*as a bright symbolic image of the future transformation*
*of matter.*

S. Semenova (Fyodorov 1982, 46)

Fyodorov, the forefather of the modern Russian visionaries, views architecture as a project of the world as-it-ought-to-be. Architecture is approached as the ultimate art which merges projection and realization of a special construction of the world and of a special constitution of the human physique capable of living in it. Fyodorov initiated a philosophical tradition that utterly radicalized the visionary endeavor of modern Russian science and art.

To build a world means to overpower gravitation. Following this maxim, the visionary-physicist Tsiolkovskii invented a rocket equipped with a self-propelled engine to launch people and to enable them travel in outer space, for he was inspired by Fyodorov's messianic vision of a future resurrected congregation of the dead that sojourns in the cosmos.

> *Mortals of all lands, unite!*
> *. . . we summon again everyone without distinc-*
> *tion of sex, age, race, class or faith and worldview to*
> *fight the eternal and mighty but defeatable and van-*
> *quishable enemy.*
> *Mortals of all lands, unite!*
> *Manifesto, 1920 (Vselenkoe Delo 1934,115)*

A communitarian in architecture, Konstantin Melnikov, was fascinated by the Fyodorovian idea of the immortality that the science of the future will achieve and the mass-scale resurrection of the dead it will undertake. Certainly the forefathers will arise. The abolition of death was a vision that induced Melnikov to design a Moscow Crematorium for proletarians, 1919; Lenin's sarcophagus, 1924; a baldachin for the funeral of Leonid Krasin, 1926; and Green City with Center-Laboratory of Sleep, 1929. In this city special tools and procedures are invented to tranquillize the citizens and to bring them into a special condition of sleep that approaches death. In Russian, *son* means both "sleep" and "dream." So, this was a lab that tested and applied collective practices of dreaming.

When working on the project of Lenin's sarcophagus, Melnikov had a vision inspired by the fairy tale of Sleeping Beauty. The story tells about a shining beautiful girl beguiled by a wicked lady into biting a poisoned apple. The piece that the girl swallows is stuck in her throat and she falls into eternal sleep. Then her lifeless body is placed in a crystal sarcophagus on the top of a mountain. Time passes and one serene day a prince who crosses the mountain sees her, falls in love with her, and kisses her dead lips. This brings her back into life, they get married and she becomes a princess. Two things are important here—the apple and the kiss. Apparently the poisonous apple stuck in the throat indicates Adam's Fall and loss of immortality. Adam was doomed to death because he bit the apple. The miraculous kiss brings back the lost Paradise. Death is dispelled and wo-man rises for eternal life. The peculiar thing in this story is that the figure of the beauty represents Eve and recalls Adam at the same time, while the prince is the redeemer himself. In this story Eve takes her deadly share of the apple by exact analogy with what happened to Adam. Then comes the Man to take out the cork from her throat, to unlock the soul imprisoned in her body and thus she is pardoned.

Resurrection means abolition of death and Melnikov expands this idea in his projects. The belief in an eventual rising of the dead makes death appear like a profound sleep. And revolutionary science will make Adam spit out the apple—his share of mortality. Melnikov imagined Lenin sleeping and he designed a sarcophagus to preserve his image intact for the kiss to come. Science will make up the lips.

Sleep close to death—this was dreamt to be the best condition for a mass-scale transformation of the human physique and consciousness to take place. In the center of the *City of Sleep* Melnikov builds an Institute for Changing the Form of Man. The whole enterprise sublimates in this center for mind and body engineering. Thus the radical vision of a thorough transformation of humankind expands into architecture. Architecture tranquillizes the zoomorphous man and brings his original human constitution to the point of ultimate change. The God-fashioned figure of Adam will be transfigured.

## Advancing Anthropo-Urgy

*We have passed beyond those periods of human history
when it was possible to think only of the psychic alteration of man, of developing in him one or another set of
ideas or moral inclinations. Along with this necessary
task of perfecting man internally, there stands before us
the problem of a more thorough transfiguration and re-
newal, of the alteration of mankind as a physical type. . . .
This creates the need for a special art bound up with a
perfect anthropology—for an anthropo-technique or
even an anthropo-urgy.*

V. Muraviev, 1923 (Starr 1978, 255)

Numerous designs of so-called garden cities were made in the 1920s, encouraged by official requests and competitions to evoke the figure of a house-plant in a city-garden where the vegetal organism of man blossoms. Melnikov, for instance, in 1927 designed and constructed for himself a house that completely resembles the cell-like dwellings in the Green City devised by N. Sokolov and M. Ginsburg. Melnikov built two overlapping cells-cylinders with numerous rhomboid openings. If not yet feasible for the entire human race, certain architects realized the vegetal vision of revolutionary architecture as their personal environment.

In Melnikov's work we encounter a strong drive toward and an exuberant application of transparent materials and elements when designing buildings and monuments representing the idea of the future world—the tower of the Crematorium and the Sarcophagus for example. This suggests a dematerialized human corporality transformed into sheer geometry and smooth surfaces that blend with the air. It suggests too, the ultimate lightness of the future being, an intuition opposite to Mandelstam's idea of architecture as ultimate organization of the opaque, dense and ponderous stone mass in a gigantic torso that utterly amplifies the athletic constitution of human physiology. The construction is not a body but a camera that transforms the physiological principle and limitations of the body.

Glass is made out of stone (quartz) that is transformed when subjected to high temperatures. Stone undergoes kind of a cremation to become pure and transparent. One could say that the glass is a stone completely freed of its opacity. This makes the glass fragile. We could use the contrast between the glass and the stone to enact more graphically the difference between the two ideas of architecture here discussed. The Revolution melted the stone opaqueness of the classical intuition for construction.

Once seized by the vision of the Crematorium, Melnikov dropped his original classical attitude and gave in completely to the revolutionary idea of architecturing the abolition of death. Compared to Mandelstam's architectural values and visions, this is a completely different and in a sense hostile system of building and structuring life-space. It would be stimulating to imagine a poem called not "Notre Dame" but "Moscow Crematorium Columbarium," where man appears not as a muscular creature made of dust and recovered from the dust but irretrievably turned into dust through a mass-scale operation in a special factory for dust. What kind of physiological orgy and athletics of the structure of a temple could we speak about when we encounter a morgue?—a morbid Mummy fortified in a grim mausoleum. The funereal mood of Melnikov's designs overpowered Mandelstam's architecture of excessive physiology.

## The Final Adam

*—Are the achievements of higher science able to resurrect people who have decomposed or not?*
*—No*

*—You're lying. . . . Marxism can do anything. What is
the reason that Lenin lies intact in Moscow? He is waiting for the science and dreams resurrection.*
                              The Foundation Pit, 133

*I am certain that the time will come when the science
will become all-powerful, that it will be able to recreate a
deceased organism. I am certain that the time will come
when one will be able to use the elements of a person's
life to recreate the physical person. And I am certain
that when that time will come, when the liberation of
mankind, using all the might of science and technology,
the strength and capacity of which we cannot now
imagine, will be able to resurrect great historical figures—and I am certain that when that time will come,
among the great figures will be our comrade.*
                          *Krasin, eulogy at a funeral, 1921*

                          *(Tumarkin 1983, 181)*

A revolutionarily justified certainty appears in the speech of Leonid
Krasin—that outspoken "god-erector" who belonged to the religious
wing (Lunacharskii, Gorkii, Bogdanov) in the Bolshevik movement that
professed spiritual regeneration and the deification of man. He was the
major strategist of the idea for a permanent exposition of Lenin's body
relic. Precisely, he was the one in charge of the whole campaign for the
mummification and the construction of the mausoleum.

During the 1920s there was a common faith in the forthcoming
ultimate feat of science that will make possible miracles on earth. The
materialistic science as the cutting edge of class consciousness was expected to accomplish Lenin's resurrection, to animate his mummy, to
give life to his temporarily stuffed body.

*Only the vision of necessity and inevitably of resurrec-
tion can explain the fact of embalming and preservation
of Lenin's body.*
                          *N. A. S-kii (1934, 145)*

At that same time, an architectural competition for designing a Crematorium Columbarium was announced with the purpose of cremat-
ing and preserving the ashes of dead proletarian bodies. This was
viewed as a preparatory procedure which was supposed to bring to a
definite end the corporal diversity of proletarians and turn their re
mains into ashes to be accumulated in a common place (later the Red
Square became the place). Designed as an antireligious measure, the
crematorium was considered to have great significance and to affect all
forms of material life. This initiative was motivated by the revolution-

ary formula of death. Cremation would facilitate the forthcoming campaign of proletarian resurrection and rise from the dust of the integrated proletarian body (the corporate body of Lenin) with a completely established class self-consciousness.

Lenin's mummy plus class self-consciousness plus science in action—these are the three elements guaranteeing the advent of the new Adam.

Here comes the radical consolidation of the bodies!

Lenin rises and communism is established in the world!

*Resurget igitur caro, et quidem omnis, et quidem ipsa,*
*et quidem integra. [The body will rise again, all of the*
*body, the identical body, the entire body.]*
                    *Tertulian, "De Carnis Resurrectione"*

### THE EVERLASTING BODY-STEM OF COMMUNISM

*When Gregor Samsa woke up one morning . . .*
*he found himself changed in his bed into a monstrous*
*vermin*

                    *Kafka*

Lenin died on 21 January 1924. On 26 January, the mourning conference of the Second Congress of the Soviets was opened, where Stalin made a speech. In it, on behalf of the Party, he pledged six oaths. The speech began with the following words: "We, the communists, are people of a special make. We are made of a special material."

Later on in the speech a recurring refrain appeared which interrupted the speech six times. In this refrain Lenin's six legacies were mentioned, followed by Stalin's six oaths. The refrain read as follows: "On leaving us, comrade Lenin bequeathed . . . We pledge to fulfill your bequest, comrade Lenin!"

The repetition "On leaving us, comrade Lenin . . . " is puzzling. In fact Lenin went nowhere because on 27 January, on the day following the oaths, he was laid in the Mausoleum. Thus he remained forever bequeathing to us and Stalin remained forever pledging to build and expand the Party space. Lenin could not leave because his body became the primal Party nucleus of power. It remained to stake out the territory where Stalin's Party imperialism was to expand.

Six days, from the 21st to the 27th, Lenin's body was laid out between the bed and the grave. Six times Stalin termed this body "leaving."

Stalin's speech began with the following words: "We, the communists, are people of a special make. We are made of a special material." The communist body does not decay!

The Mummy is the greatest communist. The stem of the Party.

The Mausoleum is the Center-accumulator mastering the collectivized people's libido.

The Mummy-stem in the Mausoleum-laboratory—this is the grand installation of modern political art and science.

## On the Day After

*Death was living standing there still and the swelling*
*brain enhanced the apprehension of danger.*
*Platonov (Vasil'ev 1982, 39)*

### THE PARTY MODERNIZES SOCIETY BY CONDENSATION AND CONCENTRATION OF THE POPULATION

*We also draw attention to the proposal for a "linear*
*city." . . . The whole city represents a single street, a*
*spine, whose vertebrae are made up of individual resi-*
*dential blocks.*

*Current discussion is not about details but about the*
*fundamental attitude toward the total character of*
*building development and the principle of design. It is*
*a question of "geometry" versus "organic."*
*El Lisitskii (1970, 62)*

The modernist visions of a Mass Man, inhabiting sun cities and garden cities, find quite a decisive incarnation in the wide communist land of the Soviets. Modernism was directly tied there to Russian universal messianism and thus became a mystery. The Party uses of such ideals were rather ingenious. Projects for linear cities were practically accomplished through urbanization of gigantic canals. Cities were designed in the form of large-scale assembly lines, or of linear transmissions for the transfer of large masses of living flesh and matter.

The working out of such dynamic communal spaces, turned out to be much harder than the building of stationary communal spaces, so-called communal flats. Professional architects take it upon themselves to design and build such stationary spaces called at that time the "new social condensers." Such a space condenses the social body, in order to make it communal. At the same time, inspired by the modern political technology of communism, there arises the idea of concentrating the communal body. The concentration camps.

Now there is a tendency to see the communal flat as a civic place, and the concentration camp as devoid of civil rights. In both cases the communal space is repressive, but it differs in its technology. Besides, in the total absence of civil rights and in the unprecedented mass inhabitation of such spaces, the practices of condensation and the practices of concentration become analogous. The condensation and the concentration of the population are two completely equivalent technologies for modernizing society.

One of the spaces, through a simple procedure, fed the other. The subjects concentrated in the camps had already been condensed in the communal flats. The communal flat is something like the entrance to a concentration camp, something like a preparatory chamber. Thus, the process of communization (read *modernization*) of society is two-chambered: first condensation, then concentration. Behind this whole process there is no hidden right, no law and order, no legally empowered and constitutionally legitimized procedure. This is a pure case of modernized social technology for the production of a supreme ideological Party article—the communal body, or the Mass Man.

Now, let us examine what the space of the condenser is and how exactly are the bodies transferred into the concentration chamber. The condenser represents a long row of cell-rooms, connected by a common corridor. At the end of the corridor are the common bathroom and the common kitchen-dining room. In the designs of official architects, such as Moses Ginsburg, for example, there is also a common library. The library, however was rarely bothered with.

The cell-room is the place for sleep. There, an individual can be alone with his or her body. The room is the only possible erotically intimate space. But that was not quite so, because the erotically intimate body presupposes a different order of society and its common public spaces. The erotically intimate body can be solely the civic one (but not the communal one) because it has a particular private presence in the social space which excites the "other" bodies. In this sense, the communal homogeneity of the bodies cannot presuppose eroticism. The communal body of the subject is forced to be intimate, for to reproduce itself it must copulate.

In the communal flat, all initiatives of the body are centralized in common public rooms and timetables. There they are trapped and sanctioned as impersonal: eating, cooking, hygiene, and so on. The common space presupposes a centralized order in which everything becomes visible except for the sexual act, which is accomplished in the dark of the room.

Berlin Dada demanded the establishment of a sexual center. Their manifesto offered a radical centralization (read *modernization*) of all possible initiatives of any possible social body. The sexual initiative is brought to light and centralized. The forced togetherness was total.

## After Creation Comes Re-Creation: The Kuzmin Project

*An examination of the charts depicting the daily routine
will reveal that I place the population of the commune in
different categories according to age. Each category lives
in quarters specially equipped for and adapted to its particular activities. As an example, I offer the schedule to
be followed by the adults:*

1. *Lights out* — 10:00 p.m.
2. *Eight hours of sleep. Reveille.* — 6:00 a.m.
3. *Calisthenics—5 min.* — 6:05 a.m.
4. *Toilet—10 min.* — 6:15a.m.
5. *Shower (optional—5 min.)* — 6:20 a.m.
6. *Dress—5 min.* — 6:25 a.m.
7. *To the dining room—3 min.* — 6:28 a.m.
8. *Breakfast—15 min.* — 6:43 a.m.
9. *To the cloakrooms—2 min.* — 6:45 a.m.
10. *Put on outdoor clothing—5 min.* — 6:50 a.m.
11. *To the mine—10 min.* — 7:00 a.m.
12. *Work in the mine—8 hours.* — 3:00 p.m.
13. *To the commune—10 min.* — 3:10 p.m.
14. *Take off the outdoor clothing—7 min.* — 3:17 p.m.
15. *Wash—8 min.* — 3:25 p.m.
16. *Dinner—30 min.* — 3:55 p.m.
17. *To the recreation room for free hour—
    3 min.* — 3:58 p.m.
18. *Free hour. Those who wish may nap—
    or better. In this case they retire to the
    bedrooms.* — 4:58 p.m.
19. *Toilet and change—10 min.* — 5:08 p.m.
20. *To the dining room—2 min.* — 5:10 p.m.
21. *Tea—15 min.* — 5:25 p.m.
22. *To the club. Recreation. Cultural
    development. Gymnastics. Perhaps a
    bath or swim. Here it is life itself that
    will determine how time is spent, that
    will draw up the plan. Allowed time:
    four hours.* — 9:25 p.m.
23. *To the dining room, supper, and to
    bedrooms—25 min.* — 9:50 p.m.
24. *Prepare to retire (a shower may be
    taken)—10 min.* — 10:00 p.m.

*The adult "communards" sleep in groups of six men
and women in separate rooms, or in pairs [former
"husband" and "wife"]. The rooms are intended only
for sleeping. The children sleep according to the age
groups. . . .*

*Family Life, in the usual sense of the word, no
longer exists. The children live independently, though,
of course, they are still able to maintain the necessary relations with their parents (through heated
galleries), etc.*

*(Kopp 1970, 152–54)*

## FEAR AND FAMINE

*Where is the exit out of the trap? The exit is clearly visi-
ble to all trapped in the hole. Yet nobody seems to see it.
Everybody knows where the exit is. Yet nobody seems to
make a move toward it. More: whoever moves toward
the exit, or whoever points toward it is declared crazy or
a criminal or a sinner to burn in hell.*
     W. Reich The Murder of Christ *(Reich 1960, 471)*

Now let us examine the transfer of bodies from one chamber into the
other. As the beginning of concentration we can see deadly fear and
famine, which is suffered by the bodies in the condensers. Famine stems
from the fact that the political economy of communism and all economic
laws lead to famine and sustain famine on purpose. Famine is the initial
organizational condition of communism. Famine, compared to the
plague, is not a calamity, but a social technology for the collectivization
and concentration of the population. Famine welds bodies together.

Fear stems from the inexorable course of the transmission modernizing society which rhythmically feeds the concentration camps with
bodies. Fear is produced by an already experienced concentration. It
welds yet again by causing trembling.

The transferring of bodies from one chamber into another happens
at night, when people are withdrawn into acts of forced intimacy. There
was a knock on the door and "they" took them away. The bodies in the
adjacent cells used to hear noises with apprehension and expected
every night to be visited by the same knock. At that time demographers
registered a sudden lowering of the birthrate. Fear decisively prevented
intimacy. The knocking on the door caused an acute castration complex.
Just as the statue of Commandant knocked on the door of Don Juan, in
order to punish him with a granite fist.

The concentration of bodies begins already in the condensation
chamber with a repressive centralization, by means of *fear and famine,* of
the two strongest urges of zoomorphous man: eating and copulating.
Thus, the communal body is deprived of all of its natural initiative. It
possesses only the Party-designed initiative.

The body was turned into a plant by means of *fear and famine*. Mass impotence set in because in the dark of night, when the body was at its bravest, man was most cynically abused. After a knock on the door, man used to be taken out of his bed where he lay in lust. He used to be taken away from the place where he had been relishing a glimpse of his boldest and most brazen dreams, the fevers of his desirous body. The central vegetative political body knocked with its stem on the door to take the animal out of its den and lead it into the sun-trap.

Thus happened Communism.

## Party Science versus Political Art

### THE RACIAL-PARTY APPROACH: THE RACIAL EYE

*Among the pictures submitted I have observed a number of works which actually lead one to assume that certain people's eyes show them things differently from the way they really are. In other words, there really are men who see today's Germans simply as degenerate cretins and who perceive—or as they would doubtless say "experience"—the meadows as blue, the sky as green, the clouds as sulfurous yellow, and so on. I do not want to enter into an argument as to whether or not these people actually do see and perceive things this way, but in the name of the German people I wish to prohibit such unfortunates, who clearly suffer from defective vision, from trying to foist the products of their faulty observation on to their fellow men as though they were realities, or indeed from dishing them up as "art." No, there are only two possibilities. Either these so-called artists really do see things in this way and so believe in what they are representing—if so one would have to investigate whether their eye defects have arisen by mechanical means or through heredity: in the former case these unfortunate people are profoundly to be pitied; in the latter it would be a matter of great concern for the Reich Ministry of the Interior, which would then have to consider ways of putting a stop to further transmission of such appalling defects of vision—or perhaps, on the other hand, they themselves do not believe in the reality of such impressions, but have other reasons for inflicting this humbug on the nation, in which case it would constitute an offense falling within the area of criminal law.*
Adolf Hitler (Jouchtmides et al. 1985, 122)

The artists discussed here are the modernists. In 1937 in Munich, the Nazis organized two parallel exhibitions. One of "degenerae art," in which the modernist artists are deliberately shown to be total idiots, especially in their particularly imbecile category, Dada. The second offered "healthy" German art, a manifestation of athleticism, of muscular eroticism, of the blue-eyed perspicacity of the German national spirit.

Undoubtedly, the problem of sight and vision is of great importance. How is it solved in this case? Since the artist paints not what is seen by the "healthy" eye, there are three possibilities: the damage is mechanical and this induces pity and is a medical case. Second, the damage is genetic or hereditary, and this case is delegated by Hitler not to medicine, but to the Ministry of the Interior. Third, the damage is mostly simulated and can be directly prosecuted under criminal law. The first two cases suggest pathology, the third suggests sabotage. Or, from another point of view, the first is physical, the latter two are ideological.

The Nazi party ideology penalizes the case of the genetic malformation as an assault against the race. The race-party criterion is the criterion of the "healthy" and the sensible, the one of common sense. Common sense is something typical of party art, because the party is the ideologically organized interest of a homogeneous mass of people, with their own common sense for the order of things, with their own organ for uniform vision, *sensus communis*. In contrast eccentricity is typical of political, not of party art, because the political act demonstrates and identifies a particular agent with his own acute partial social interest. The fighting political agent publishes his own interest differently from the party agent. From the standpoint of common sense of the party agent, the publications of the political agent are always subversive. In this case even genetic malformation is treated as subversive, that is, as a political phenomenon, because genetics is loaded by National Socialism with a party sense.

Let us get back to defective vision. We have spoken already of the machine eye, of machinism in general, and of the collage principle of modernizing normal sight. The modernist principle of representation is just such a machine for reorganizing vision. In this sense, modernism does not represent, but reorganizes the organic principle of sight into a mechanical, technological, geometric one. The modernist eye reinvents the sight. Of course, from the point of view of normal vision, and the more so when it is loaded with ultimate party sense, this eye is faulty. The spectator looking at the canvas, does not find a re-created reality there but a set of prostheses belonging to the handicapped eye of the painter.

The racial-party approach elevates the organic into an ultimate value and considers as an assault against it any attempt to attach prostheses. This same Nazism deifies the machine, but only as a means of exhibiting the will of the organic. The mechanic as a willful extrapolation of the organic. The modernist idea of radical replacement of the naturally organic with the machine is a sabotage. In this sense, the party ideology of National Socialism is the opposite of the modernist one. Hitler attacked modernism as a phenomenon which is political in its nature.

Nazi art is open to the *sensus communis*. And common sense dictates the following—art organizes the vision and virtually represents the organics of the visualized. A painting does not represent merely some object or body, but the principle of its natural organics. If the object-prototype is slightly marred, then its image brings back its organics. In this sense, defective images are not possible in art, because art itself is a regenerative, not a degenerative activity.

The problem of party censorship lies in the depiction of the "representable," because party truth is connected to it. The image is neither an actual empirical prototype, nor the thing immediately represented on the canvas. The representable offers the ideal integrity of the image. The representable cannot pose technical problems, but only ideological ones. In it resides a truth lying beyond any empirical manifestation. Artistic mastery lies in the act of making the image ultimately transparent, so that the representable can stand before the eye, clearly and fully.

Such censorship is a party institution, not a political one. It does not come from any concrete political agent who is in power and who says what can and what cannot be published. This censorship is not a political institution, defined as a state structure. The censorship which guards party truth works by giving form to thought and imagination.

Party censorship is not a separate institution which permits one type of thought and prohibits others. It acts as the structure of thought or sight. It poses the organically fundamental state of things, and not their politically defined state. Such a censorship does not censure the phenomenon, but the person who gives birth to it. It does not outlaw the painting, but the person who has seen the real that way. On the contrary, political censorship prosecutes the phenomenon, the thing born. Ideological party censorship prosecutes the nature of the birth. Because it prosecutes persons, and not phenomena, it is not defined as a state institution, but acts through the organs of security.

Party truth liquidates political art, because it liquidates the political personality in general: either everybody in the party or everybody in the camps!

## THE CLASS-PARTY APPROACH: PARTY REPLACES CLASS

Now let us discuss the class-party approach as similar to and different from the racial-party approach. The one liquidated political art in

Germany, the other in Russia. And everything began with Dada and the Proletcult.

The racial-party approach stems from the organic unity of "blood and soil" as a genetic source of national purity and the historical mission of the race. Things are not so simple with the class-party approach, because the Communist Party claims to be one thing, but is, in fact, quite another. But let us begin elsewhere.

*Literature must become party literature. Down with non-party writers. Down with the writer-superman.*

*The literary work must become a building block of the organized, planned, united . . . party work.*

*Writers must necessarily enter the party organizations. Publishing houses, reading rooms, libraries—all of these must come under party control.*

*In defining the borders between party and anti-party writing, the criterion must be the party program . . . its statute.*

*Lenin (1980, 14–19)*

It is evident from Lenin's thought, cited above, that the Communist Party idea, even as far back as its prerevolutionary state, has been developing as an imperial idea. The new emperor is the Party.

What Lenin wanted in 1905 was actually accomplished in 1932 at the writers' conference, where formalism (read *modernism*) was totally liquidated and the omnipotence of the new Party truth in art was proclaimed. Thus the writers entered the Party. Those who do not, go to the camps. Thus the political person in art is liquidated. Party truth flourishes and recruits its shamans and priests. Party truth or Party justice (*pravda*) becomes the basis of the new Inquisition. True art is justified by Party art.

In 1920 Lenin devised an attack against the Proletcult. The motives were that in its ideas and practices the Proletcult was decisively independent of the Party line and Party interests. And that was true, because the Proletcult was the actual political Proletarian art of that time with its ideology and action program, with its own organizational structure independent of the Party. Not Party literature, but Proletcult is the politically representative art of the proletariat. The ideologists of Proletcult were all suppressed by Lenin and thrown out of the Party. We are not discussing here the extremism of this art and its idea in general. We have already discussed that in relation to Dada. Here, the important thing is that a structure was built, independent of the Party, which represents the proletariat itself. But the Party liquidated all this, because it subverted and competed with its political representativeness. Everything which might undermine the political representativeness of the

Party was incriminated. The peasant, for example, a political person whom the Party does not represent, was totally stripped of rights, if not physically exterminated with administrative executions and deliberately caused mass famine. The deprivation of rights goes as far as the peasant's lack of a passport, without which he cannot leave his village. He was actually not a citizen and could not represent even himself, because he was totally illegitimate from the Party point of view.

Thus a new class was formed—the Party oligarchy which held the entire power. It was not the means of production, but the means of power, which organized the new communist social relations. Who holds and who reproduces political power through its own means? Not the proletariat! The Party represents the interest of those who are the immediate body of power—the so-called *nomenklatura*. The Party membership mass organized on horizontal principle is a totally fabricated phenomenon. But Party interest continues to fake a proletarian class interest and constituency. Party art vigorously continues to express the workers' presence in the world. Why: The laboroid imagery in no way represents the virtual social interest of the Party oligarchy.

Why doesn't it glorify itself? It remains hidden, invisible and untouchable. It acts as a lizard, which detaches its tail as soon as it is stepped on. Because, from the point of view of civil law and order, from the point of view of the politically public agent, this oligarchy is illegal. So Party art represents a fabricated political agent: the proletariat.

The question of the legality of the Party and Party policy in art is central. In his article about Party literature Lenin elaborates this question. At that time, before 1917, the Party and all its publications are illegal. Legal publication are non-Party. But there comes a time when the Party begins functioning legally and then all possible publications have to become Party ones. Coming out of illegality, the Party usurps the whole press and there is no need of any law for the press (because law is necessary where there are different political interests, i.e., different political agents). In a state of all-encompassing Party policy a law is unnecessary because the only differentiation is Party/anti-Party, and that differentiation is ruled upon by the program and statute of the Party. The statute of the Party is the very law which constitutes the possible relations. In this case, the state actually does begin dying off, because the Party takes up its functions and gradually replaces it.

Not until now have there been preparations for legislating a law of the press and not only of the press. Only now has the possibility of the existence of political agents outside the Party been admitted.

Intra-Party life is conspiratorially closed from the point of view of the state and the few laws there are in it. But it is legal, nevertheless.

Lenin begins, but does not develop his thoughts on the legality of the Party. That the Party is legal does not prevent it from developing an internally conspiratorial life, with its own structure, discipline and secrets. Any change in the power structure happens in the form of a conspiratorial plot.

The existence of the Party is legal, but it is illegitimate in holding and executing the whole power, which it has actually usurped through conspiracy. It actually represents the interests of the Party oligarchy and no one else, it is not sheathed in a law, voted for by free citizens. It does not possess delegated rights from a multitude of citizens, it endows itself with power through its program; the state constitution is only a repetition of this program. The territories, where Party interests act most strongly, are not regulated by law, because there no other political agent can exist, or have a legal status. The law is possible only where there are relations between independent political agents.

The Party suffers from a chronic insufficiency of representativeness, that is, of legitimacy. From here on it begins to liquidate and take away the rights of anything which might compete with it, or subvert it, or sabotage its representativeness. It liquidates modern political art, precisely because it competes with its right to represent the proletariat. The Party collects a great mass of members, creates its own simulated sociopolitical interests, which only it can represent. It invents a class-party approach, which should define good and evil and other tricks, so that the real class, the real interest should sink into conspiratorial darkness, since it cannot have public forms (because it is illegitimate, and rules over the public, visible world through ghosts). The proletariat as a class, as an actual political agent, has long ago disappeared, because the structure of social relations is ruled not through ownership of the means of production but through possession of power and by the degree of initiation into the Party conspiracy.

The phantom of proletarian class interest continues to exist as a means, not as an end. The class-party approach is the means of production of power. The trick with the Party policy of art is in the following—that which is given to us as Party criterion, that which we have caught and hold on to as a Party truth is only the tail of the lizard. The lizard has long ago escaped unharmed. We hold on to words, phrases, slogans, hammers, tanks, images of laboring hands and brave blood donors, of bridges and golden wheat, with the ontological certainty that we are holding on to the whole new and daring communist reality. But this is only the lizard's tail. Whoever does not wish to hold on to the lizard's tail and pretend to be holding the proletarian hammer in hand, is liquidated. The lizard comes back to feed itself.

The racial-party approach of Nazism was clear. National Socialism came to power in Germany through a legal procedure and for a short while it really began to express and represent the German national mind which was inspired by it. The party is legal and its structures are not conspiratorial. The power which it holds becomes legitimate organ of highly organized national interest.

The class-party approach of Bolshevism, the internally conspiratorial structures of Party life, the publicly simulated structures of Party truth—this drenches the whole physical space of society with permanent Revolution.

The mummy of the Leader! Why does a civic legal political power need mummies?

The class struggle and the dictatorship of the proletariat become the main ideological alibi for the liquidation, which the Party carries on against all evidence and witnesses of its own illegitimacy.

The class motive and the racial motive of the totalitarian parties liquidated modern political art. The two motives are completely different, as I have attempted to explain. The link between them is that both have worked out their own technologies and ideologies for the liquidation of possible political agents, who by definition represent non-party interests.

Presently, when the serious work on the analysis and criticism of the class party empire in art and public forms of life in general is forthcoming, we have to take into account what Dada really is, what a scandal this crocodile is, what a saboteur it is, that Party crushed it in panic with a ferro-concrete fist.

## The Hologram World

### SOCIALIST REALISM
### AS A CONCRETIZATION OF COMMUNISM

Any imperial power uses and abuses theater as the most powerful metaphor of the world. For it makes the world a stage and all people actors who play different roles as to their appearance as well as their disappearance.

The theatrical visions of Evreinov, Meyerhold and Stanislavskii follow.

## Evreinov: Revolution-Transformation-Digestion.

*The art of the theater is pre-aesthetic and non aesthetic
for the simple reason that transformation, which is, after*

*all, the essence of all theatrical art, is more primitive*
*and more easily attainable than formation, which is the*
*essence of the fine arts.*

*Evreinov (Golub 1984, 54)*

Evreinov, one of the most special, subtle and extravagant Russian modernists, theater directors, historians and theorists, right after the Revolution was seized by a revolutionary rush, euphoria and jubilation that made him deviate from his peculiar aristocratic aesthetics. Evreinov was the ideologist of monodrama, of the theater for one-self. He professed an experimental performance of suicide, thus challenging the limits of life. He carried to an extreme the artistic platform of the Crooked Mirror Theater by writing and staging the play *In the Stage-Wings of the Soul.*

It was Evreinov who directed a grand mass-revolutionary spectacle called *The Storming of the Winter Palace.* It took place on 7 November 1920 in the real space around the Winter Palace to commemorate the third anniversary of the Revolution. It was an integral part of a grand project for serialized mass-staging of the Revolution as Deliverance of the Toil that started on 1 May 1920 with the *Mystery or Hymn of the Liberated Labor (Misteriia ili Gimn osvobozhdennogo truda).* The project reproduces the principles of the medieval Mystery play in that it overwhelms the entire city life and space and transforms the everyday world into a feast of the All-Mighty Force that dominates the human cosmos and manifests through its lurid/carnival transfiguring. The major principles of this revolutionary Mystery are: simultaneous action on different platforms, multiple presence of the protagonist and the antagonist, real city environment, fusion of the two worlds—on and off stage.

Evreinov wrote about *The Storming:*

An artillery shot sounds. Light breaks through the white platform and illuminates the worn-out stones of the olden hall. On a dais, the Provisional Government, with Kerenski at its head, accepts pledges of loyalty from the former dignitaries, generals, and financiers, as the band plays a false Marseillaise. On the red platform, against the background of brick factories, the International starts up, and to this music, individuals in the throng and then hundreds of voices yell out: "Lenin! Lenin!" . . . While those on the white platform spend their time at all kinds of meetings, the proletariat on the red platform begins to unite around its leaders. . . . The Provisional Government is protected only by military cadets and the Women's Battalion, and it flees to the Winter Palace. Then, the windows of this last citadel of Kerenski light up. The Reds have now organized their own military detachments and point the Winter Palace out to each other. . . . Machine guns crackle, rifles fire, and the artillery thunders. . . . There is a continuous din for three or four minutes. . . . But suddenly, a rocket goes up and everything instantly becomes quiet, so that the air can become filled with new sounds. A chorus of 40,000 voices is singing the International. A five-pointed red star starts to light up above the darkened windows of the Winter Palace. An enormous red banner is raised above the building itself. . . . The show is over and the Red forces begin to parade. (Gorchakov 1957, 149–50)

The universal transformation is a basic revolutionary trope that builds this grand performance. Evreinov had never been a leftist revolutionary intellectual. What probably amazed him was the emerging theatricality from the flux of Revolution. Theatricality—this is a key concept in his aesthetics. Theater must not be a presentation that isolates events by arresting and confining on the stage the mighty surge of life. Theatricality is a representation of entire life in transformation. And the Revolution occurred to him as a spectacular performance of this principle. In order to be more precise we have to stress that theatricality is an aestheticized transformation. Per-formance stages trans-formance.

Evreinov considers theater as a special act that precedes art itself. Art is termed to be a formation of unique works whereas theater transforms all things existing—fictional or real, unique or profane. Once it comes into being, the theater equally manifests through art and through everyday life.

Transformation represented as a stage prior to any possible formation—this was the agenda not only for Evreinov but for Russian art critics and philologists, for the "formal school." They were influenced by Goethe's original theory of metamorphosis of plants. Goethe wished to reinvent the Ur-plant (the primordial stem) by tracing back the multiple metamorphosis of various plant species. He declared transformation prior to any formation. He regarded formation as end-stage of the transformation. Goethe's idea was epigraphically presented in Propp's book-manifesto about the morphology of fairy tale. As a matter of fact, these epigraphs are completely omitted in the English language editions.

There is a particular symptom that occurs often in Evreinov's writings, namely his propensity to use gastronomic imagery. Eating, food and digestion often sustain his argumentation:

Reason, science . . . the satiety of the people, toil-hardened hands— what was left to us except for this? . . . We lost our taste for life. Without seasoning, without the salt of theatricality, life was a dish we would only eat by compulsion. (Golub 1984, 53)

Beauty is such a tasty sauce, you could eat your own father if he were garnished with it . . . (56)

> Just as in the field of the subtlest gastronomy the connoisseur is
> satisfied only with the cuisine prepared by his own personal cook, so
> in the realm of theatricality "the theater for oneself" is the last refuge
> of the refined soul. (57)

His major contribution to the gastro-physiological vision is the play called *In the Stage-Wings of the Soul.* It was "set inside a man's body and depicting his giant internal organs on-stage. . . . The actual set, designed by M. P. Bobysov, featured a gigantic spinal column upstage. A large heart, lungs and other organs moved rhythmically in time to the music" (Golub 1984, 42). The intestines were designed as a stage-machine which allegorized "the wings of the soul," made the soul act and prompted its impulses. The point was that the physiological transformation of the organisms preceded and determined any possible activity of the psyche. Precisely the inner set of the body sets the stage where the selves of man will act. The digestion/metabolic machine of the body generates transformation. Digestion transforms the devoured material into life-supporting substances. Then comes metabolism to transform substances into impulses and reflexes that brings psyche into life.

Evreinov translated the metabolic principle of the organisms into metaphoric principle of art. He merged metaphoric with metabolic impulse. The work of art recurs to him as organism in transformation and the act of creation as digestion. Theatricality manifests precisely the threshold where a work of art turns into a digesting machine that consumes life.

Evreinov saw Revolution as a grand campaign of political digestion. He staged the revolutionary metabolism of public life as Universal Mystery.

What is important for our investigation is the fusion of biological with creative function of human being and the advancement of a graphic opposition between formation and transformation of the systems, political and natural. In this respect modernist art performed Revolution as an act both metaphoric and metabolic. The major idea was that the political performance is immediately rooted in the biological transformance of mankind.

## Meyerhold: Box, Biomechanics, Constructivism

*How do we set about molding the new actor? . . . If we*
*place him in an environment in which gymnastics and*
*all forms of sport are both available and compulsory, we*

*shall achieve the new man who is capable of any form of*
*labor. Only via the sports arena can we approach the*
*theatrical arena.*

*Every movement is a hieroglyph with its own pe-*
*culiar meaning. The theater should employ only those*
*movements which are immediately decipherable; every-*
*thing else is superfluous. . . .*

*Ecstasy is the notorious inner experience, the*
*"authentic emotion"; it is the system of my teacher Kon-*
*stantin Stanislavskii . . .*

*Meyerhold (Braun 1969, 200)*

Revolutionary modernism treats the psyche as bourgeois and obsolete. Only the physique matters because it brings into life a vehement transformation. Meyerhold brought the extreme of the revolutionary physique in the theater. The classical theater based on dramaturgy and naturalistic settings was ruined by the all-absorbing surge of virtuoso acting, gymnastics and pirouettes performed on kinetic sets and platforms. He worked together with prominent constructivists and futurists. He tested in his theater-laboratory various ways and approaches toward perfection in acting and maximizing the capacities of the human body. He installed the body-actor in a geometrical environment with kinetic constructions. He advanced the installation of special contraptions and machinery on a series of platforms, thus erecting industrial surroundings for exercising theatrical athletics. He advanced in theater the techniques of an athletic toil that operates with futuristic apparatus. The unbound labor was staged as an ultimately precise and easy acting. A body-acrobat revolves and flips over the trapeze operating with bizarre implements. This demonstrates the eccentric cooperation between revolutionary body and gear in the process of athletic toiling.

Meyerhold transformed the stage into an area which brings together gymnastics and geometry. He turned the actor into a toiling gladiator, equipped with futuristic armory, who suddenly changes into an acrobat launched in the stereo-metric space and who finally turns into an eccentric clown upon landing. He inspired the creative mind of his disciple Eisenstein to advance this circus aesthetics in the brand new art of film, where it found a stunning application known as the "montage of attractions:" This is how through aesthetic intervention revolution designs and triggers a new vision of reality. The new politics of labor re-tailors vision and resets bourgeois perception by bombarding and invading it with optic shocks.

Meyerhold named his aesthetics "biomechanics" which fully expresses its original essence. He mounted the astonishing Centaur of

Revolution made of maximized biology and maximized technology, of masses and tools, of bodies grown together with contraptions.

Modernism professed a technological as much as biological transformation of humankind. There is no given paradigm to comply with and to mold things according to. There is only Revolution in action transgressing the given. Art transforms given reality. It does not reflect any already set reality. Reality of the future is in art.

Meyerhold's aesthetics is traditionally viewed as the opposite of Stanislavskii's system. Stanislavskii's system (notice the difference in name, we relate Meyerhold to aesthetics and Stanislavskii to a system), was later appropriated in the Soviet theater as the official system for actor training and acting. This system instructs you how to comply with the pre-given forms of reality by disciplining an organic behavior on stage. It trains you to build and perform the authenticity of your psyche on the basis of the given.

The eccentric physique of Revolution was arrested. An ecstatic psyche was induced through socialist realism to act in accord with the "given circumstances" of the already established Real socialism.

## Stanislavskii: Given Circumstances, Organic Authenticity and Character Building

*The system (of Stanislavskii) is one of the tools by means of with theater implements in practice the method of socialist realism.*

*The aesthetic principles of Stanislavskii's system were finally set up as a result of the complete exploration of the new socialist reality. . . .*

*Stanislavskii's system stems from the living reality and enacts on the Soviet stage the art of the authentic life.*

*N. Abalkin (1950, 281)*

We consider Stanislavskii's system an important field for our investigation, because it stands for the so-called Real socialism. The system of Real socialism recognizes and proves itself through Stanislavskii's system of acting and staging. The term *Real socialism* designates a specific stage on the way to complete concretization of communism in life. On this stage social reality still makes the Ideal deviate. On this stage the people still need instruction and correction.

Stanislavskii's system instructs the actor how to build a part in the play. The same instruction applies for the everyday subject who had to build an adequate presence on the stage of Real socialism. Historically speaking, the system was enforced as official only after Real socialism was established. It dates the final consolidation of power around the all-mighty Stalin after the "Congress of the Victors" in 1934. This means that Stanislavskii's system was not developed expressly to enforce Party principles in the realm of the arts. It means that the system was only later officially recognized as the Party-approved one.

This would justify a *quid pro quo* reading of the system: when the system says actor we read subject. When it says stage we read public space. When it says "unbroken line of action" that pervades any performance and assures its integrity we read Party line. When it says an "ensemble" that acts according to a consciously worked-out discipline, we read society. When it says "super-objective" or "super-assignment" that sums up various strivings and wills, we read the historical mission that lines up society for the relentless march towards the end. When it says "given circumstances," we read that status quo that public actors have to introject.

The system trains the actor not to "present" a character-mask or a body-hieroglyph. The expression "theater of presentation" of abstract ideas through eccentric body language labels Meyerhold's aesthetics. Stanislavskii developed the opposite idea for an actor of "the inner experience." This actor builds the character in his/her self and out of his/her self. The actor works out a suggestive appearance that becomes an organic physiognomy and inner echo of the "given circumstances" and not a political hieroglyph or abstraction. The character is developed by the actor through the actor's own psyche, and then enacted as organic body behavior and never postured as abstract figure.

The "super-objective" and "the through line of action":

> *Super-objective.* That is the inner essence, the all-embracing goal, the objective of the objectives. . . . In carrying out this super-objective you have arrived at something even more important, superconscious, ineffable. . . .
>
> This striving which expresses the essence of creativeness, is the *through action of the role or play.* . . . The through action is the *active attainment of the super-objective.*
>
> Thus the process of playing your part consists of composing a score for your role, of a super-objective and of its active attainment by means of the through line of action.
>
> (Stanislavskii (1961, 77–80)

The presentation of self in the given circumstances according to the super-imposed-objective—this is the agenda of the system. Ultimately this system instructs you to introject the super-objective that has been assigned by the director and projected upon the end of the play as its ideological conclusion. It trains you to get used to the pre-established *status quo* (the so-called given circumstances) and to internalize it by building an individual system of motivations. The actor (subject) has to experience the assigned role through his/her inner self and then to recognize and motivate it.

Submit your-self to the given! Devote yourself to the super-objective! Then apply the techniques prescribed by the system and develop the appropriate behavior.

Here comes the application of the "method of physical action." Through repetitive performance of "simple everyday actions" the actor adjusts his/her physique and emotion to the *given* circumstances and commits his/her entire being to the *super-objective.* The actor experiences the "external circumstances" through the inner self and thus accumulates an "affective memory." The actor recalls this memory on stage and affectedly performs the action "as if" it spontaneously originates caused by the unique encounter of the external and the internal condition of life. Thus the actor achieves authenticity in acting. The actor presents no hieroglyph but an authentic being raised and cultivated through his/her very self. Performing authenticity: this is the ultimate accomplishment of acting.

The actor is an actor for he/she creates authenticity that has appropriated the "given circumstances" and "super-objective." Besides, the actor is an actor for he/she stands on the stage for a specific audience. The audience authorizes, approves or disapproves of all that could take place on the stage. When an actor masters the role this utterly gratifies the audience. The system says "audience"; we read "public'."

## The Triple Identity of the Actor

The actor is a publicly secluded being. Stanislavskii views the actor as a special being who acts "as if" alone on the stage but in front of an audience (the public). Thus the actor brings the intimated "character" from inside out and lays it bare for the public eye. The watching public is utterly excited when the actor opens the stage-wings of his/her ad hoc fabricated soul. The actor's role is to make himself ultimately transparent and penetrable to the quick. All that is basking in the lights of the stage is authentic, for it is rendered transparent. Authenticity goes with visibility and public recognition.

Make yourself transparent in public and gain your social authenticity! Otherwise the theater (public life) cannot take place.

The actor has to build an organic appearance on the stage. This means that a plausible and comprehensible causal relation is to be established between "the external circumstances" and the inner "affective memory," between the given and the mind, between stimulation and reflection. The actor is assigned to build a "second plane," an "inner monologue," a "film of the inner vision." Acting reveals on the stage a personal organic Inside for the anonymous public gaze to view. This gaze comes from the dark to authorize the hara-kiri of the psyche and to feast its eye on the disemboweled intestines.

The basic intuition is that the act of art does not transform life. The idea of transformation is completely abandoned. Acting does build an authentic character-organism upon internalizing the *given* and *super-objective*. The actor at first builds into his/her self a part that is to be publicly demonstrated afterward. This understanding overturns the value judgment of art. If we assume that the work demonstrates in public what was already built inside the psyche of the author, then, if we judge the work we in fact judge the self of the author. The work stages the public face of the author. Wrong work means wrong authorship, wrong inner condition, wrong innate organic. The personality of the author cannot be politically discriminated from the work itself. In-versely, it is fully committed there. When you incriminate the act, you arrest the actor.

While we are building the system, it built us up!

## The "Magic If"

*The real world . . . has always been the apparent world*
once again.
     *Nietzsche,* The Will to Power, 566

Let us consult Nietzsche. He endeavors throughout his works to prove that the *world of appearance* is the original one and that the *real world* is fabricated by the acting will to power. The world of appearance is per-ceived through our senses, whereupon we receive the only genuine and authentic picture of reality. The real world is erected on the ground of appearances and is structured by the acting power.

The real is a composition of appearances. It is a constellation of vi-sions. The real is a fabrication authorized through power. Hence a con-clusion: the original world is granted to our senses as virtual reality. The so-called real world is that same, originally apparent world taken *once again* through the rhetoric devices of the ruling ideology.

Nietzsche helps us see the radical shift: "the apparent as if real" that comes into life through theater. We are going to argue that precisely this generic shift, inaugurated through the system of acting here discussed, makes the holistic picture of real socialism possible. The system of the real socialism is a composition of visions, projections and party enthusiasm charged with enormous political power and thus made real. It is an appearance sustained by the generic shifter "as if real" plus a population instructed to act accordingly.

*If* "this" was "that" and "I" were "him," then . . .

The "magic If" is a major metaphor that designates the basic principle of the authentic acting in Stanislavskii's system. The same philosophy "as if" brings the generic shifter that turns my-self into another-self or transforms one set of reality into another one and the play becomes "as if" for real. Upon applying the shifter, the actor becomes able to put himself authentically in any fictitious (given) circumstances. The execution of the magic "as if" shifts the "inner experience" from the track of illusion on the track of reality and renders it authentic.

Activating the "magic If" starts the system itself. The theater begins and ends not within a plot, but with enacting or terminating of the generic "as if." To establish the initial conditions for a performance, you need somebody on the stage who acts "as if" he/she is somebody else and you need people who see this "as if" it is happening for real. The performance is over once there is nothing on the stage to initiate and nothing off the stage to sustain the shifter "as if."

A general conclusion follows: Within the system the real faces no revolutionary transformation. Rather, the apparent is made real. The entire commune is made drill the "as if" shifter.

## The "Fourth Wall"

*The Fourth wall! . . . This is Columbus' egg!*
                    *Evreinov (1976, 11)*

The "Fourth Wall" is another major metaphor of the system. Stanislavskii spoke of the so-called stage-box. Theater takes place in a two-chambered space: stage and audience. Here the special set-up, not the principle of acting, provides the magic tool. This is the missing Forth Wall of the stage-box that opens both chambers (the dark and the lit up) one into another. Thus the magic of the spectacle is made possible. The theater takes place because the Fourth Wall is "as if" erected, or we may say: because it is "as if" demolished. The spectator cannot enter the stage because the Wall is "as if" there, but the spectator can watch thereinside because the Wall is "as if" removed. One may say that the spectator encounters a transparent wall. The same is effective for the actor.

Actors act "as if" alone and turn their back to the audience, something that violated the classic theater code.

This "as if" presence of the Fourth Wall is a generic situation for the theater. All that matters appears on stage behind the transparent wall. All that is left outside or put away from the stage receives no authorization or recognition by the spectator. It is considered a foul reality that is drained away from the public gaze.

The only difference between this system of performing and Real socialism is that the latter has a transparent ceiling. The supreme Spectator watches from above the stage and His all-pervading gaze is vertical.

The public transparency opens up into the dark and lets a Gaze penetrate.

## The Arrested Reality

*Meyerhold set against the psychological disclosure of the role on stage. The "constructors" of the eccentric theater did the same. . . . They announced . . . "from emotion towards machine, from affective acting towards trick."*

*Formalist theater does not love life and despises man. . . . It appeared to the formalists that in the Soviet theater the creating of the truthful actor would go in two parallel directions: creating a mind-acrobat and a body-equilibrist.*

*Life itself buried these ideological acrobats and equilibrists.*

N. Abalkin (1950, 293)

In a book about Meyerhold, *Temnyi Genii*, Iurii Elagin (1982, 391) formulates a very important principle of Real socialism. When a prominent individual or a celebrity makes a serious ideological mistake, the severe criticism escalates so long as he/she is at large. Even the most brutal criticism indicates the fact that the criticized individual is physically at large. The arrest terminates anything that could possibly be a sign for the existence of that individual. Their very presence in the real world is arrested.

Meyerhold was arrested in June 1939, right after his participation at the All-Union Conference of the Soviet Directors, where Vyshinskii was the key speaker. At that time Vyshinskii was appointed Procurator-General for his great success in concocting ideological accusations and setting up political trials against the "Trotskist conspiracy" and the "enemy with Party-membership card." Apparently Meyerhold's speech did not appeal to Vyshinskii and aggravated Meyerhold's bad reputation for being a major "formalist" and an extremist plotting against the Party leadership. Meyerhold disappeared. Shortly after this his wife was found in her apartment atrociously murdered and mutilated. All that could make this name present in public was annihilated, obliterated and incriminated. He was fully wiped off the face of Real socialism. He was purged from the Soviet stage and the system took over completely.

State terror had a special function, for it made socialism Real. The mass purges opened up a different social space known as GULAG. Gulag was sanctioned as foul reality that did not belong to the Real.

Gulag made the bright Real lugubrious. The population was actually terrified by the glamorous visions released by the works of socialist realism and ideology. Those visions appeared in a lurid aura, for they figuratively recalled the criminal, ferocious and brutal realm of Gulag. The growing pile of socialist imagery testified to the fact that people were being purged and the cesspool of Gulag expanded.

The ubiquitous socialist realism displaces Gulag but precisely for this reason it stands for it. A total presence of socialist realism would signify nothing but a completely displaced Gulag.

## Gorkii: Socialist Realism Enacts Being as Action

*Myth—this is an invention. Invention means to abstract from the given reality its basic meaning and to incorporate it into an image. Thus we obtain realism. If, however, we elaborate further this abstracted meaning with the probable and the desirable, and develop the image, we thus obtain romanticism, which lies at the foundation of the myth and which agitates the revolutionary attitude toward reality—an attitude that practically changes the world.*

*Bourgeois society completely lost the ability to invent in art. Bourgeois romanticism—does not excite imagination, does not sharpen the thinking.*

*Gorkii (1980, 357)*

Shortly after the 17th Party Congress known as the Congress of the Victors, on 17 August 1934, Gorkii delivered his notorious speech at the First All-Union Congress of the Soviet Writers, which was accepted as the manifesto of the new method of "socialist realism."

The major task of this speech is to prove the historical inevitability and necessity of socialist realism to come by building a genealogy of labor and its different sociohistorical forms of organization. Labor transformed the vertical animal into a human being, it developed the whole set of conditioned and unconditioned reflexes into a consciousness able to reflect and change reality. The consciousness is an ultimate organization of matter achieved through labor. Unfortunately labor was enslaved, and society was broken down into classes. The class of masters developed a "false consciousness," fabricated gods and composed religions in order to subdue the mighty urge for justice of the toiling masses. Social systems based on exploitation of labor buried this progenitor of consciousness under a heap of forgery and fabrications. And communism comes to unbind labor, to dump the junk heaped up by bourgeois culture and rehabilitate the original power of consciousness to imagine, create and invent.

Here comes a specific assertion about art: realistic art abstracts the principle of reality and composes an image that makes this principle visible. Realism exposes the code of reality. Juxtaposed to this, the contribution of socialist realism seems the ultimate one. It does not merely reflect the present principle of reality but refracts it and brings it to its final perfection. Socialist realism implements in a realistic image the very project for changing reality. Thus the "socialist" image constructs reality by developing knowledge of its change. The socialist image is a dialectical conjunction between reflection and projection.

The forth-coming communism be-comes real in the socialist art of the present. Thus socialist realism is more than reality itself. It is the real, because the real is current reality mastered through the project of its change. The real is a master-piece. It is an inviolable perfection that is made proof against any current deviation. The real is a grand mold that was sculpted out of reality.

## Reality and the Real

Socialist realism is not simply a method of writing or conceiving reality. It testifies to the real. It figures society as a whole. It affects the entirety of the world, its constitution and building principle. Socialist realism enforces revolutionary ideology and makes the basic class interest manifest in the sphere of imagination.

The real is not limited to the empirical mass of reality. Neither it can be exhausted by the teaching. The real is like an all-embracing cast that solidifies reality according to the Party political forecast. The real is a special fortification of the social organism that shields it from outside and keeps it mastered by the Party code inside.

The real is ideologically justified and impregnated against any degeneration of reality or abuse of power. If there occurs a deviation of that kind, the political language terms it "error of the growth" and it gets corrected by the Party code. Real socialism is a self-correcting organism. Each party congress restored the violated code of socialism and designed a new five-year campaign for retrieving the real back into reality.

Reality could degenerate. The real ever regenerates. The mission of socialist realism turned out to be a constant regeneration of the real in the conditions of a progressing historical degeneration of reality. It is this gradually accelerating discrepancy that undermined the communist instruction of the population. A general mental and physical malfunctioning of the population derailed the engine of communism.

## Political-Party Reality

*Current discussion . . . is a question of "geometry"*
*versus "organic."*
                              El Lisitskii (1970, 62)

An anti-organic and pro-mechanic idea was developed by Russian political modernism—wings like constructivism (Tatlin, Lisitskii, Rodchenko, Stepanova), Proletcult (Gastev, Eisenstein), futurism and the biomechanics of Meyerhold. This idea defines the technological as a precondition of any further biological transformation of humankind.

During the 1920s the political art maximized its projects and visions through demonstrative negation of the "organic integrity of nature" and the enforcement of a "montage set-up of man" and a "machine-made society." Political modernism confronted the classical idea for organic unity of the work of art. New visions took over: a society devised and tested in laboratories; the work of art as a sharpened incisor cuts out and fragments society according to a radical political sociometrics. Political modernism extolled the mechanical replicas of human organs. The natural determinations of the body were proclaimed extinct. Society was no longer contemplated in organic terms but rather in industrial terminals.

The 1930s marked the complete victory of Party ideology over the political art of Russian modernism. During this period the Party appropriated the whole public and private space. The Party lined up society. The organizational consolidation of socialist realism abolished the compound body of political modernism (consult Lenin's notes against Proletcult that launched the first general antimodernist campaign).

Party-determined social body merged its political and its natural function. Real socialism liquidated any idea that emancipated any natural properties of man that could challenge its class determination—genetics was rejected and the Lisenko doctrine was developed.

The Party ideology retrieved the ancient intuitions of "organ," "organon," "organic." Tautology was established between "nature" and "techne," human-born body and man-designed machine, hand and instrument, and so on. Hand and sword grow into one organ.

Modernism projected *the political integrity* of society as a machinoid entity assembled contrary to its natural condition.

Socialist realism enacted *the Party integrity* of society as a radical fusion of the political and the physical and declared psyche to be a side-effect. The Party conducted through communism an arrested modernism.

## THE HOLOGRAM OF COMMUNISM

## Pyro-gramma and Holo-gramma

### *Pyro-gramma.*

Modernism lauded the flame-throwers as blazing ejaculators which burn out the natural joints, ligaments, sinews and muscles of the body and proliferate the superhuman semen. It lauded the acetylene torches that weld together the new political construction of the body. Modernism lauded all these red hot pokers which scrutinize and probe the body, cut it apart and weld it together again, thus making it capable of incredible feats of labor. The flame-thrower transforms the obsolete religious congregation of people into a politically reunited assemblage of the people. Cutting and pasting, fractures and prostheses: these are the visions of the unique political surgery and orthopedics of a modernized society.

Revolutionary art demonstrates an amazing social pyro-technique which brands the body and inscribes on it the heraldry of its new political condition. The radical constructivism, expressionism, Dadaism of the world designed blaze bursting furnaces, synthesized new materials, molded new elements and welded the knots of the new world. The modernized world is built out of pyro-grams, has a pyro-grammatical set-up and the political body that inhabits it has a blue-print physiognomy.

### *The Holo-gramma*

Party policy in art abolished the "attractions" (Eisenstein), the "biome-chanical body" (Meyerhold), the politics of decoupage and collage and the whole gear of political modernism. Stanislavskii's system was erected as a Party sanctuary. Contrary to the political modernism, the Party ideology and socialist system imposed a total instruction that created an organic integrity of the social body. Socialist realism sculpted the world as an integral whole. The work of socialist art miniaturizes the Real.

Socialist realism devised the holograms of communism. The work of art was perceived as an ultimately organized whole (*holos*), which radiated communism and rendered the current Party design visible.

The hologram is an image projected into the real space of life. The *holo-gram,* contrary to the *pyro-gram,* does not represent a dismembered social body put together again in contrast to its natural organic principle. The hologram radiates a three-dimensional phantom, which generates illusion for physical presence. The hologram does not transform reality. It projects a *reality effect.* The integrity of virtual reality cannot be violated or damaged by anything physical. Physical intervention has no effect. The integrity of the hologram can be attacked and violated only if the optic and the beam that project it are damaged. This is why the socialist realism that molds holograms cannot be refuted. Its visionary integrity is untouchable.

The Red specter walks through walls. It inhabits a different space where only "Fourth Walls" are erected. Those who try to catch it are doomed to smash their face against reality that frames them.

The Communist Party controlled society by building a total visionary space and confining the population in there. The bodies lined up in the hologram could not knock it down. Being there, they could only testify to its presence.

Communism is a reality effect. It is a visionary topos projected into space that can only be recognized as a topical and not as a historical phenomenon. Communism is not a historical materialization of capital, nor is it a socioeconomical formation. It is a topos, organized beyond the frame of history and thus an utopia or simply the end of the world.

The Mummy materializes the Red specter and represents the congenital body of communism. Hence, the Mummy is the Party testicle.

## Terror in the Holo-gramma

In-deed communism was built up as socialist realism.

The entire body of industry was a formidable compound that materialized the communist visionary endeavor. Through toiling in the factories and marching by the Mausoleum people comprise the body of the vision. The Fourth Walls of society were dematerialized by the all-pervading Party gaze. The magic "as if" agitated political jugglery. The population was interned in a visionary space experienced "as if" real.

Real socialism was suspended from the Forth Wall and transfixed by the shining and vigilant Party gaze.

The major task was to provide the population with a cogent motive to proliferate and to feel accomplished in the virtual reality. How did the Party raise the people in the grand hologram of communism? It came up with a very simple technique: it opened special stage-wings of reality and interned there some of the actors. People relentlessly disappeared; they got lost, never to return again. People were devoured there in the tunnels and dungeons of the KGB, in the devastated space of the Gulag. A brutal force emerged in the hologram to kidnap people. This created a double condition for Real socialism. The virtual (official) reality was experienced as prosperous and blissful because the other one was suffered as a punishment and damnation. People were being constantly kidnapped and kept "there" as hostages for the others, who remain on stage to feel prosperous and to make the hologram real.

Going back to Nietzsche, one may say that the true and just world is the one that enables you to sojourn in it. The wrong world annihilates your ability to exist.

Visionary space became real precisely because the Party made part of the population disappear through the stage wings of nothingness. Thus only the world of the Party appearance proved to sustain existence. And the hologram turned real upon alternating with nothingness. Real socialism made appearance alternate with disappearance.

If you want to curb, for instance, a Party activist like Kalinin you put his wife away as a hostage. If you want to make Stanislavskii's system a general communist instruction, you make Meyerhold disappear.

Terror turned the tool that implements ideology in the realm of psychology and physiology. Terror concretized vision. If you want to make the paradise real, open an inferno. In this respect Real socialism was particularly subtle. Socialist realism was totally established and no legitimate tool for building an inferno was left. Whoever dared to verbalize the Inferno turned up there, disappeared.

The dissident literature developed a counter-endeavor. It brought the inferno back into the domain of creative language, made Gulag present against the background of real socialism, transferred hostages back into existence.

Thus the fight between socialist realism and Gulag subrealism was not a fight for a dominant artistic method or aesthetic principle, nor even for an adequate epistemological approach, but a fight for the true communist ontology.

Fight for reality: that is what art is all about in Real socialism.

## Visions Materialized

The Mummy was installed in the center of the system, then monumental fortifications for the Mummy were erected and the terror was conducted throughout the entire substance of life.

The architecture of communism is petrified ideology. Communism unfolds a terrifying visionary space and the major concern of power is to provide the terror with a real object. So as not to disorder but to socialize, terror has to spring not from an apparition or a spooky corner of life. It has to spring from the real itself and to sustain its principle.

Through mass repression, the Party provided itself with a terrifying body. Thus terror acquired a real aggressor and omnipresent surveillance—a real eye. The gaze cut through reality like a guillotine. And then comes the day when Mummy, People and Party reunited in a common orgy during the solemn parades in front of the Mausoleum.

All the power techniques of Real socialism performed one thing: they reified visions and exhausted the excessive quanta of "affective memory" accumulated by the population. Thus Party power constantly prevents the population from going completely mad.

Terror in the hologram of communism induces suspense as the dominant feeling. Communism is forever suspended. It is perpetually in historical ordeal because of errors or treachery. It is ever in the act of leaping supported only by the parables of the Teaching. Each new stage impersonated by a new leader proclaims the preceding development wrong and historically failed. The population perpetually apprehends the emergence of a brand new vision or unprecedented formula which is going to do away with the old one. A new brave impostor (leader, judge and executor in one) is about to enter any moment, to disperse the macabre apparitions and to put straight the Cause, the Way and the Fist. The population imagines power as an opaque zone moved by endless plots and machinations that pulsates between heroism and treachery.

## Montaigne's Proceeding

It is amazing how Montaigne composed his *Essays* using the verbal decoration of his famous philosophical attic. He used to inscribe sentences and aphorisms on the wood beams in the ceiling of his tower. He, so to say, coated his ceiling with slogans, instructions, truths, maxims and imperatives. And when he was writing his *Essays* he was taking down in the book the propositions engraved on the beams. In a certain sense the word of the *Essays* had already been present in the interior that surrounded the act of writing itself.

Socialist writing and composition proceeds in a similar way. Surplus production of words is the virtual objective of the system, which made the public space look like a scrapbook stuffed with Party resolutions. Words were launched into the public space to substitute for the vanishing goods.

Philosophy or any ceremonious manufacturing of words had a pivotal function in this system. The public space was propped up by slogans, sentences, appeals, imperatives produced by the Teaching. The same verbal corpus was displayed also on the pages of newspapers and books written by numbers of ideologists. They followed the same approach as Montaigne. From the Façades of the public space, Whereon only the Party had the prerogative to write, they took down words, slogans, instructions, planting them in books as magic seeds.

The verbal front of reality constantly expands. The entire set of magic words progressively changes and thus the Party perpetually reconfigures its historical appearance. This makes possible the rising pile of books which interpret the self-adjusting Teaching. The verbal volume of communism expands because the Party appearance grows.

The word uttered by the Teacher haunts the total ideological space of society. Lenin is present through eternalized word and mummified body too. His word establishes the real. His body is real, in this space packed with restless phantoms and oratorical resounding. It represents the ultimate merger of ideology and physiology.

The Mummy is the original socialist realism.

## The Hologram of Communism

Real socialism changes as a whole and ever remains a whole. It is a self-recovering totality. It is a self-improving fabrication. Socialist realism established a virtual integrity exactly the way a hologram projects a reality effect.

Real socialism enacted the dictatorship of the visions begotten in the Party underground. It springs up from the underground fortification where the Mummy is preserved. The real is impregnated against decay and exposed there for a perpetual watch. Subjects at large line up there to watch it and their enlightened gaze keeps the vision intact. This grants eyes with a special faculty and mission.

The Mummy Lenin is the hologram of communism.

# 3

## Induratio Spatii of the Revolution

# Red/Black: Poetics of the Conspiratorial Space

*. . . on the platform of the communist decoding of the world.*

Dziga Vertov (1984, 50)

## Red Square

*To Moscow! To Moscow!*
*Chekhov, "Three Sisters"*

The ability of the reader to envision what he/she reads, to see it in the mind's eye as on a map—flat and graphic—is of utmost importance for the correct interpretation of all that follows.

### TOPOGRAPHY

*So we refuse to let Lenin be falsified by art.*
*A. Rodchenko (Bowlt 1988, 253)*

Red Square, June 1989.

The correct position of anyone who stands in Red Square in Moscow would be to face Lenin's Mausoleum, which represents the symbolic center of the Square. From this position Moscow's central space is arranged in the following way: the Mausoleum is in front with the Kremlin behind it; the Passage or the Central Department Store is to your rear; to the left is the Cathedral; in front of it—the Place of Execution; behind it—Hotel Russia; to the right—a large museum building, behind which is the Inter Hotel. From this point the Hotel can be reached through a long tunnel under a gigantic empty space with automobiles speeding over it. (See Map. 1).

Map 1 has not been drawn from the above point of view; but from the viewpoint of a person standing with his back to the Mausoleum. This is a privileged perspective since it is taken by the Mummy itself, if we imagine it standing up. This is also the viewpoint of leaders and teachers who ascend the rostrum of the Mausoleum on solemn national days to face the exulting crowd below.

### THE CAPITAL

The Mummy is laid underground in the Mausoleum with its head pointing towards the Kremlin Wall. If I may use a masonry idiom, it is "the cornerstone" (Matthew 21:42) which props up the whole construc-

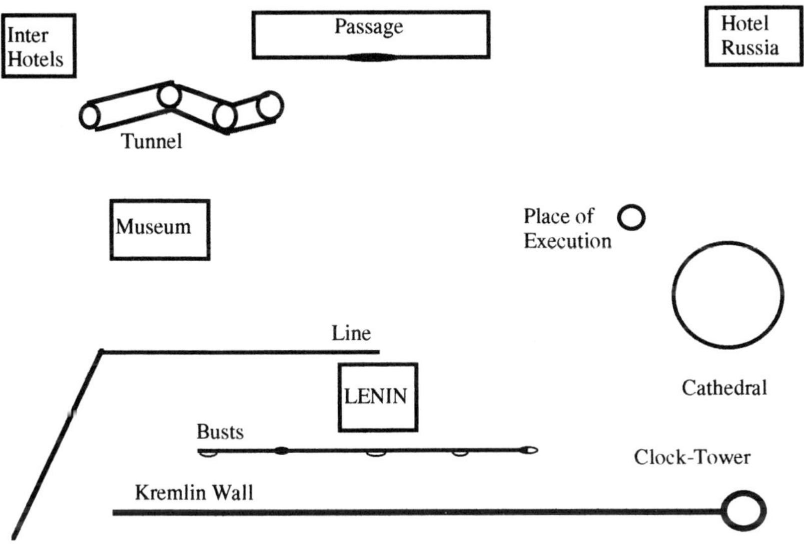


Map 1   Red Square

tion of Kremlin and signifies the ultimate, that is, the primal symbolic point of the entire space which opens above and around it.

The Mummy is the vertex of the primal corner which opens up the huge space of the Kremlin, Red Square, Moscow, and the entire USSR.

The name LENIN is engraved on the Mausoleum; this is one of Vladimir Ilich's conspiratorial names. The Mummy bears the name of the Great Conspirator. It is the capital that props up the structure of the Brave New World. It lies beneath a glass lid, carefully guarded. Its right hand is clenched into a fist, as if it was clutching the cap of Ilich only a while ago.

### THE EGG

It is worth noting that the Mausoleum is not situated against the Kremlin's entrance but rather against its front wall. Facing the entrance with the clock is the Place of Execution. Thus, the Mausoleum resembles a giant swelling on the front wall, having locked inside a mighty abscess.

The Mausoleum is a catacomb. Something like a huge egg, buried half-way in the ground which, like any ellipse, has two foci: an upper one, the Rostrum, which governs the time of solemnity in the city; and a lower one, the Mummy, which governs the time of mourning in the city.

Mourning erects solemnity. Mourning emanates solemnity. In times of mass exaltations and parades the two foci merge. The egg-ellipse becomes a perfect sphere. Solemnity is extremity of mourning.

The Mausoleum as a special gate does not open the horizontal dimension of life. It makes up-down pitch of life possible. Down is the ventricular and up, the bulging shape of the Mausoleum-Egg. A womb turns into phallus. The Mausoleum is an androgenous structure.

The clock-tower, the famous Kremlin clock, is a projecting metamorphosis of the Mummy. This is a clockwork-mummy. The numbed body turns into a machine. The constant, the immovable Mummy strikes and thus cuts out the communist timetable of the city. The rhythmic spasms of a womb conduct the pulsation of life.

### THE WOMB

The womb has engulfed the dead body without being able to decompose it. It is underground, where the original symbol has descended to endure change and decay. Mummy manifests the ultimate *induratio spatii* transgressing any time-duration. It opens the world and in this sense is the solid threshold that terminates history, time and mortality.

### THE PARADE AS A CONTRACTION

The womb is shaken by contractions in solemn cycles. An eruption ejects the symbol rising and shining. Thus the womb begets the time of solemnity in the lower depths of its funereal chasm. The womb contracts its interior, which makes the square become erect and elevated: the Rostrum. The Mummy rises in the figure of the General Secretary who waves from the Rostrum and the mourning procession turns into exultant parade. The opaque becomes sparkling. Thanatos—Eros. The Black—Red.

The Egg-Mausoleum molds the vertical, the sacred space of the square. It represents the point where the space is fractured and fit together again as a miraculous joint which makes the city enact a mysterious spectacle.

### HAMMER, SICKLE, FIVE-POINTED STAR

The Mausoleum is a Centaur—an ever galloping creature assembled by the figures of mourning and solemnity, of Black and Red, of the Reaper and the Blacksmith, the Hammer and the Sickle: Life and Death.

Just as the Mausoleum is present in Red Square, so is the state emblem present on the Red flag. The state emblem is a coded Mausoleum. The five-pointed star is a Gordian knot of angles. In contrast to the six-pointed star, it cannot be dismantled into triangles. In this way it represents a primal indivisible symbolic device. It is composed by a single unbroken move of the hand drawing a line that locks together a figure which cannot be disassembled. There is the utmost Party consolidation of geometry: ultimate in meaning and wonderful in fashion.

### OPPOSITES: THE EYE VERSUS THE FINGER

The double cosmos of the Mausoleum infects the surrounding space.

1.   The *Kremlin* is right behind the Mausoleum: the official space. The Kremlin is a museum. The museum creates a strict separation between the exhibits and the viewers. The exhibits represent a detached, mummified reality, which makes present and visible the sacred values, such as Nation, History, Glory, and so on. The essence of the exhibit subordinates by definition the body of the viewer. The exhibit is elevated and detached from the currents of life. The museum carries the surge of the past over the actual.

Besides being a museum, the Kremlin is the headquarters of power. Power rules the exterior of the country and stores in its interiors evidences and traces of this rule. The interior of power stretch out as far as we confront traces of its presence. The world proletariat and its representatives have access to this interior. In the far margins of the exterior are interned the ignorant mass of ostracized profanes and excommunicated social residue, deprived of the sacred initiation and recognition by power.

The Ruler does nothing but magnifies His ostentatious power behind the jagged walls of the Kremlin. The visitor is urged to imagine Him by reading the traces deposited by Him in the museum. The museum is an allegorical space which bears the traces of something absent—the unfathomable Ruler. The museum is a wonderful device making Him imaginable through His accessories. This stimulates political idolatry and fetishism.

2.   The *Passage* is on the opposite side of the Square, that is, across from the Mausoleum. Contrary to the official space of the Kremlin, here is situated the promiscuous zone; the public dissipation; the guts.

The gigantic gate of the Passage gapes right opposite the Mausoleum. It is a huge concavity in the corpse of the building with two winding staircases like two windpipes. This orifice opens up the gulping soft interiors of the Passage. People crawl through its interiors. The space is segmented into a multitude of cells and passages between the cells where the ultimate act of promiscuity is performed—trading by means of a universal medium of exchange, the Ruble. The bacchanalia of the objects changing hands is governed by the universal medium of exchange, money. The capital grows precisely by the bustle of bodies and goods, by this frantic eroticism of touch and taking possession of objects.

There, in the Kremlin, the law of life is made up. Here, in the Passage, life breaks out as a bacchanalia. The objects and bodies are not exhibits anymore, they are commodities. The commodity and the buyer obey the principle of mutual acquisition; they stick together in mutual affect. The power which runs this whirlpool is immediately tangible and visible: the Ruble.

3.   *The Ruble:* the name literally means coined. It is the most perfect and ultimately efficient sculpture.

The capital symbol is engraved on it. Often, Lenin's capital poses there. The ruble is a special ambivalent token. One of the sides represents the sacred value through the image of the Mummy. The reverse bears its pragmatic value expressed in numbers.

The Ruble welds together the tokens of the grave and the promiscuous order, the spiritual and the carnal, the ocular and tangible dimention. It is a joint made of icon and number, a Centaur. It is the point of refraction of the two codes. It is a device which incites both, worship and corruption. It constantly holds us between the Museum and the Passage, that is, in the Square.

The Ruble is a sculpture that people feel and look at. It is a key that opens both, the horizontal and the vertical space of the Square.

4.   *The Cathedral* rises by the Kremlin. Nowadays, it exhibits, it does not perform services. The cathedral resembles a huge rudiment that testifies to a long-gone collective life of the city. This exhibit encloses the congregational space, the liturgical function of which, at present, is taken over by the Mausoleum.

5.   *The Hotel* is situated right behind the Cathedral and on the other side of the Square there is another hotel. The Hotel is also a communal

space but a dissipated not a disciplined one. Just as the Cathedral is a common home for the congregation, so is the Hotel, only it is not sacred but vulgar, not high but low, not grave but lenient, not spiritual but carnal.

The Hotel bustle looses the city prostitution. At twilight when the Mausoleum closes, just before the guard changes, the prostitutes crawl out of the Hotel and head for Red Square. At this hour it is full of strangers of all sorts who by definition demonstrate a promiscuous attitude.

The prostitutes are dressed in somber black attire, moving with a sluggish, extremely decorous gait, devoid of any aggression or exhibition of insolent flesh. Like mourning figures coming out of a requiem, they gather in front of the Mausoleum. After the changing-of-the-guard ceremony, unless they are dispersed by the militia, they walk away just as phlegmatic.

The city Eros performs mourning ceremonies. The Red is disguised as Black. The Mummy makes the commune of the prostitutes bow to it. Thus the global city space in all its segments manifests the presence of the Mummy.

6. *The Tunnel.* Red Square is linked to one of the hotels by a long tunnel, winding like a labyrinth. The intestine. The sewer.

Walking back, the prostitutes slink into the underground, and there below the level of the Square, in order to throw off the burden of the mourning pose, twist their bodies erotically. Around the orifice of the intestine a lecherous crowd is bustling, and with the descending black of the night this central erogenous zone of the city blushes. The invading voluptuousness of the night makes the rim of the orifice blush. The Red and the Black join together once again. The Centaur gallops.

Below the level of the Square, is safeguarded the dead numbed body of the Mummy and there also hides the feverishly alive body of Eros. The open space of the Square performs their embrace. It is a figure of their fearsome kiss.

7 There is a place on the Square which breaks the pattern described above. This is the round *Place of Execution.* It is situated in front and a little to the side of the Cathedral and doesn't fit into any of the symmetries on the Square. Slightly elevated, it is situated across from the entrance to the clock tower. It is a rudiment of a former center of the Square.

Once it focused a sublime publicity. This was where the decrees were announced. This was where death sentences were executed. This was where the body of power exposed its sublime visibility. Now, this huge bare stump represents a rudimentary center of the former congregational order of the city.

When the Mausoleum was erected, it reordered the symbolic dominants of the Square. This happened after the death of the Great Conspirator, of the leader and founding father of communism. The removing of the center changed the codification of the Square. It replaced the tokens of the earlier, Christian congregation with the attributes of the actual Party conspiracy. The congregational code of life was replaced by a conspiratorial one.

### THE CONGREGATION

The Cathedral and the Place of Execution (now exhibits-rudiments) once legitimated the congregational space at the center of which the Tzar-*Pater* stood. The Place of Execution and the Cathedral were the sublime rostrums of His double, secular and religious power.

The congregational space was structured in some primal legendary past. Its spatial totality and principle of integrity emerged, supported by both mighty metaphors and divine icons. Congregational life built a liturgical concord of people fortified with powerful values, metaphors and sacramental attributes of the age-old tradition. The congregational space reflected a transcendental Intelligence and incorporated the divine Decorum. Thus it proved to be beautiful and blissful.

### THE CONSPIRACY

It is a concord, but in the sense of a plot, a cabal. The Party conspiracy arose within the framework of the original congregational order at the moment when it disintegrated because of its growing economical and political debility. The Party plot emerged to ruin the congregation. The conspiracy represented an idea for radical change of the social order. The brand-new social organism was identified in terms of a Party ideology by demolishing the age-old tradition. This calls for a new principle of concord to be established and get a firm foothold conspiratorially outside law and tradition.

Unlike the congregation, conspiracy manufactured entirely new metaphors and attributes to authorize itself. Its legitimacy was finally enforced by the Revolution.

### THE PARTY NITZSCHEANISM

Dionysus in his bacchic excess destroys Apollo's statues.

Precisely in the forms of conspiratorial life the will to power gains utmost expression. It is cast on the stage of the eternal neurotic *becoming*.

Party life performs radical deliverance of the will to power from the ever-lasting age-old value, *being*. Party life represents the highest manifestation of the actual. The Party realizes its own interest as arbitrary tampers with the age-old values, hammers and reaps, cuts out reality with the sickle.

Party ideology is the most efficient tool for satiating the inventive force of the will to power. The Party reinvents the past since it is the well of tradition, it stands prior to any becoming and transcends the actual. The past solidifies the immutable being of the tradition. In the struggle with the Apollonian past the actual Party Dionysism struggles with its greatest rival. For the purpose of victory, it performs artful manipulation: it merges before and after.

The past was declared no longer an absolute before, no longer un-touchable formation of being. Past was transformed and retold in various Party narratives concocted for the purpose. The past was represented through strategically restored rudiments which were meant to solve certain problems of the marching Party actuality. The significance of the past was always ad hoc. The past was an apparition released by the current Party plot (narrative) which stimulated the public imagination and formed certain mass representations. Therefore the past was never prior, it was always an effect of the active Party interest.

The ever-changing rhetoric-strategy of the Party plot took over life, devising new metaphors and dismantling the old ones. The Party was constantly usurping the public space with new words. Reality had to adjust perpetually to this enormous verbal influx into it.

The one who controls names, controls reality.

Language constantly rapes reality.

## THE MUMMY

The ingenious device of the conspiratorial power is the one that shapes public life into an everlasting mournful wake or a triumphant parade and thus exhausts the excessive will for Revolution. This is the Mummy Lenin. Ilich remained with us forever with his words and his body. Thus the mummified conspirator perpetuates the underground plot for seizing and controlling power by detecting and punishing traitors.

The Mummy incarnates a titanic will to power. This is Vladimir Ilich eternalized in his conspiratorial name Lenin.

### THE COMPOSITION OF THE MUMMY

*The Egyptian mummy* is a dried up body impregnated and fortified for eternity by a mask-shield. It is the sacred sign for a life present There-beyond, in the Other World. The mummy of the Pharaoh is a magic device which conjoins the corporal and the spiritual omnipotency of his power.

*The mummy of the saint:* Long before the coming of death, the saint dries up his body applying special ascetic procedures and exercises. The fact that after his death the relics of the saint do not decay is a proof of their sacramental essence. The relics are a substance blessed by God, charged with enormous and miraculous power.

In contrast to this, *Lenin as a mummy* is much like himself. He isn't dried up, there is no mask, no days of sacred exposure and no days of taboo. The Mausoleum has open hours, not a holy calendar. Any religious suggestion that there may be something of Lenin There-beyond besides that which is Here, is eliminated. His perennial body is a sign of the *omni-here-present* Party power.

We already mentioned the great certainty that overwhelmed minds concerning the forthcoming resurrection of the Fathers' bodies. The Second Coming of Lenin is sustained by science and is going to be brought about by science. He is the only Father with a body absolutely preserved.

The Mausoleum is a marvelous catapult constructed to launch Lenin back into the living world, as the Cross is a special bow nailed together to launch the Messiah beyond the world. The Mummy is a marvelous pupa. Like a butterfly, Lenin will take off some day from his own mummy.

Later, Stalin was also laid next to Lenin and remained there for years. This is how the conspiratorial power demonstrates its fertility, as it reduplicates the symbolic devices which guarantee its being here forever. The multiplication of mummies demonstrates that power is in progress, that it deposits over the territory more and more signs-mummies of the Omnipresent Party.

The Egyptian mummy and the Soviet mummy codify the public space in a contrasting manner—in a congregational and a conspiratorial order. Power is either granted or seized. It comes along by a divine authorization order or is seized according to an ad hoc conspiratorial plan.

### THE MUMMY AS A SIGHT
### FOR THE COMMUNAL EYE OF THE WORSHIPPER

*I am a mechanical eye.*
*I, a machine, show you the world as only*
*I can see it.*
                    *Dziga Vertov*

1.    A mourning line of worshippers over a kilometer long waits in front of the Mausoleum. The perpetual wake is on.

The line crawls slowly, enters the Mausoleum, exits, passes along the Kremlin Wall behind the Mausoleum, where remains and ashes of many a conspirator are buried, and disperses in the crowd. This mourning ceremony enacts the conspiratorial assembly of the Soviet subjects. The mourning procession sinks into the lower depths of the Mausoleum to see the Grand Conspirator exhibited there. Thus the subjects are initiated into the secrets of the Party plot which will fold the face of the earth anew.

The mummy is the *perpetuum mobile* of the Party plot.

2.    But there are other days on the Square, days of jubilation not of mourning. The mourning ceremony transforms into lined up and parading masses. The class demonstrates through marching its involvement in the conspiratorial plot against the bondage of capital. The mourning is dispersed by euphoric chanting. In the features of the Black, the Red breaks forth and ruptures it. The supreme organ of power raises on the rostrum to hail the exulting crowd and to screen with its corporate body the graves of the heroes lined along the Kremlin Wall.

3.    The Party life makes Eros break out in the features of Thanatos, jubilation in the bosom of mourning. The exulting people tread over graves. The rostrum is the top of a gigantic coffin. Everything emerges here and now at once. Thus conspiratorial space embraces the Mummy.

4. The original body in this space is the body through which time does not pass, nor does history. It alone is the primal engine of history. It is undecomposable symbol solidified for eternity. Decay as a trace of time is arrested. The principle INDURATIO SPATII of communism originates right here.

The Mummy deposits time out of itself without being subject to it. Its corporal constitution is comparable to no other body in this space.

5.    No photography is allowed inside the Mausoleum. The machine eye is banned. An eye emancipated from the code of the Mausoleum is not allowed to see it. The camera is a machine that manufactures images, not a naked eye consuming them. The Mummy is a special device that codifies and tunes up the communal vision. It charges the eye with intuitions for real and fake, for truth and falsehood. The machine eye is a foe of the Mummy because the Mummy is the prototype that has no copy and cannot be technically reproduced. A copy would make the suggestive appearance of the Mummy preposterous.

6.    The Mummy is a miraculous freak of nature. The body is dead but is not rotten. It is dead but this is precisely how it provokes the triumph of life. It is deadly pale, but the gazes that touch it redden its surface.

7.   The Mummy is the deepest threshold where the Red world breaks in the Black one. The Mummy burns in the gazes and illuminates minds crossing over it. The Mummy dreams extinction. The eye of the worshipper, wherein the ultimate sight has stuck, also needs relief. This is why right behind the Mausoleum there is a long row of graves with busts. In the bust the dead face preserves its own image without being its very self. Decay is replaced by the hardness of the rock on which the features of the living face are engraved. Behind the graves with the busts, right into the Kremlin Wall there is the long row of urns where the ashes of the heroes are kept. There are no images here, only names engraved on golden plaques. Cremation has purged mortality and its tokens—the decaying flesh and death mask. A sheer heroism, totally extracted from the corporality of the heroes, is built in the foundation of the Kremlin Wall.

8.   This is how the ultimate body achieves extinction as it gives up its face and substance to the busts and the ashes. This represents the ceremonious immuring of the Mummy in the city corpus.

The same happens to the feverish eye of the worshipper. Having seen the Mummy, then the busts, then the hundreds of names of heroes, the eye introjects and subdues the ultimate sight which shall master the vision from now on.

The mourning procession that descends down into the Mausoleum undergoes an initiation which bestows the eye with an underground intuition of Party truth and justice (*pravda*), and the body with an underground togetherness and solidarity.

9.   Certainly this is valid for a body immediately involved in and subject to the Soviet space. For the stranger the Mummy is the ultimate stunt. It could also be termed—the ultimate souvenir never to be acquired. The stranger is always an agent of *oculus ex machina* because his body remains firmly estranged, that is, not involved in the conspiratorial space. The stranger has a photographic eye.

*Tell me frankly, what ought to remain of Lenin:*
*an art bronze,*
*oil portraits,*
*etchings,*
*water colors,*
*his secretary's diary, his friends' memories—*
*or*
*a file of photographs . . . photograph records?*
*I don't think there's any choice.*
     A. Rodchenko (Bowlt 1988, 253)

# The Appearance of the Whole Is Figurative

## the political/fictional reality

## The Political Overhaul: Dismantling the Collage

The USSR was assembled from a multitude of nationalities and peoples, with the idea for an unprecedented collective life of the working people, liberated from oppression and exploitation. People were before long moved about and interchanged according to the will of the supreme Party body, with the strategic purpose of depriving them of their age-old title to autonomous existence. The identity between nation and territory, people and land was abolished as a remnant of the past, as a prejudice. Nations were forcibly prepared for an entirely new life in the universe, for an immediate expansion on and eventually out of the Earth. Thus the geopolitical face of the Soviet state was transformed into a gigantic Dadaist collage, assembled on the Earth but not rooted in it. The state-collage exists only if there is a strong hand to pull it together.

In the programs and practice of Dadaism the collage is viewed as stunning encounter of two or more incompatible realities on a plane drastically inappropriate for that. Nothing fits anything according to the major principle of radical discrepancy and incongruity. The objects are fractured because in the collage each of them breaks up upon contact with the next one, thus aggressively ending in it. The one-sidedness of each piece is maximized. The collage captures the promiscuous touch of crashed objects hurled in the space. A broken object uses the closest fragment as its own prosthesis. Bodies are mutilated by the very act of their paroxysmal touch. This is the magic orgy of crippled objects and bodies. The collage holds ruins together.

In the course of time the state-collage atomized, with its broken and damaged realities, millions of people and thus the original idea for a hitherto unknown collective life collapsed in the face of a simple problem—the inability of humans to survive in the collage. So, pulling the state-collage together is mere Party Dadaism.

The Mummy is of great importance in the collage space. The body of the Dadaist (Lenin) is the capital piece in the collage—the cornerstone. The Dadaist personally plunged in the collage he had concocted, and consolidated it by his own Mummy. Thus the collage became a total work because it appropriated what had been radically outside it—the body of its own engineer.

The body of the painter transfixes the picture as its ultimate stroke.

## The Mummy Stalks in the Margins

If you leaf through Lenin's *Philosophical Notebooks,* you will realize at once that they demonstrate the principle of collage. This very book, by virtue of its arrangement, is a bold conspiratorial device.

The Great Conspirator read books. He took notes in the blank margins of those books. He filled margins with words. He impregnated with words the void that holds the text together by its own "blank" lack of words. Thus Ilich transformed the blank margin into a Party institution which administrates the correct meaning and understanding of the text.

The official publication of the *Philosophical Notebooks* made the margin the Institution for Detecting the Meaning and Correction of the "False Consciousness" of the Author. Lenin's words patrol in the white margins of the books. They supply the only correct reading of the text and the proper label of the author. The Party word landed in the blank margin takes over the free space of meanings that roam there at large.

The book itself is a collage. It was concocted with words cut from the books, affixed to their Party understanding, and deployed in the margin. Apparently, the collage is framed by the words cemented in the margin. The margin duplicates the Mausoleum. The words that impregnate it mummify the meaning. They frame and stuff the text.

This book has a particular status in any library. In it, unlike any other, the reading Mummy parades.

## The Fictional Reality: The Literary City

In the tourist guides for Moscow and Leningrad (now St. Petersburg) there is a section entitled the "Literary City." Unlike, say, "Revolutionary Leningrad," "Literary Leningrad" represents a scene of events which never took place in reality and which are only described in the Russian fiction. Thus the city's corpus bears tokens and traces of pure fiction and the tourist in this city may hallucinate freely in a common hallucinogenic space.

Let us examine the following case: The author, as well as the character, have lived in the same street. But the tourist is also on this street now. The body of the tourist brings the present tense on the street. In contrast, the author carries its past, while the character inhabits it both in the past and in the present. The character is a perennial specter roaming the street.

The eye of the tourist sees double. It sees the street both as "historical reality" and as "fictional actuality." Thus two dimentions of life are established: The historical and the fictional one.

*The museum* exhibits the "historical reality," usually the home of the author where everything is preserved exactly the way it was at the moment of his death that is, at the moment when a home might become a museum. Even the clock shows the exact time of death. The clock marks the vanishing of life in history. The museum aura created around the objects by their conservation rejects the body-presence of the viewer and recognizes only his/her watching eye. This aura makes realities distant and estranged, makes life something that is arrested, which now only appears present but is phenomenally not present, and the viewer has no body in this reality. This is how man builds the past.

Just the opposite is true for the *fictional* actuality. It conjures up sheer hallucinations. It is ever continuous in the present and is left to the natural course of life. It is not arrested and preserved in a museum. The house where Raskolnikov killed the old woman, for instance, has not been repaired ever since. Now it is not what it had been back then, at the time of the murder, because the murder never really happened. But it does happen fictitiously at every single moment. Up the staircase of the house, hidden in dark corners lurk reckless young men ax in hand. At the flat where the event has not really happened, a knock is often heard and the people who live there open the door annoyed or enraged by the constantly returning murderer. Not to mention the groups of tourists with whom the staircase is teeming. So many years have passed since the time when Raskolnikov, the character, was reported to have killed an old lady in this house, yet no one dared touch or rearrange a thing in it. Time flows unbroken.

The fictional actuality does not need a museum to become distant and estranged. On the contrary, it is estranged from the moment of its invention and must be made familiar. This is why everyday life itself is allowed to act through it. This is how the fictitious event gains reality and the body of the tourist enters freely its space.

The museum fictionalizes current reality. It arrests and envelops it with the aura of the not-here and not-now and so excludes the body of the viewer. This procedure generates an objectively visible past.

Unlike the museum, the traces of fiction attain actuality since they incorporate the body of the viewer.

Man contemplates the real but dwells in fiction.

The ax-men do not go to any objective past. They go to perform the fiction, to make it actual. Should the building be whitewashed, the flat vacated and turned into a museum and the staircase marked with signs reading "Toward the apartment of the Murdered Old Lady," then no ax-men would hide there for no one goes to perform the real past. All go to see it.

The city space is split because of a double codification—merging or separating names and things, literature and reality that make the body participate or suspend it. Until the body is communicated or excommunicated from the sight, it cannot be determined whether the city life imitates fiction or fiction imitates the city; whether the city has an objective past or only a present distanced intentionally "as if" into the past; whether the past is an original order of things or a particular design of present things.

The position of the Mummy becomes special when considered in the perspective of this double code of the city. Apparently it is the actual body. But this body has not passed into history. It does not represent a historical or mythical past, otherwise it would have been marked with specific vestiges of an arrested time. The Mummy is not a relic of an individual who was once alive: Lenin. It is the ultimate Party condition of that same individual in the present.

The Mummy is nothing else but itself, therefore it cannot be a vestige of a past life, nor of a fictitious current life. The Mummy stands beyond the principle of real and fictitious, beyond the code that splits them.

The Mausoleum is neither a museum nor a place opened for the everyday flux of life. The Mausoleum is a stage where all possible codes are paralyzed. The Mummy effects in the body and the eye of the viewer a complete stupor. The sublime sight is suffered as an initiation shock. Here, in the original catacomb of the city, the codes of life cease to function. Because the One appears.

*The portrait includes both presence and absence . . . the*
*real excludes the absence.*

*Pascal*

The Mummy is the maximum of presence, totally excluded absence. The Mummy is the Real.

## A Parable

The burning pain makes the hot metal and your hand merge into one organ. Your distorted face is that organ. The face is the scene of the pain.

### THE COLOSSAL, RAMBLING SPACE

## VDNKh: The Colossal Decor.

The colossal space of Moscow is known as VDNKh. The overall style of this space is an Empire of steel and soil, of hammer and sickle.

The colossal architecture accommodates the colossal products of working-class hands. Muscular giants and full-bodied maids, frozen in timeless postures on the roofs of the pavilions, carry goods in their hands.

Labor, having once jumped out of Pandora's box, is the ruler here. It stages an universal spectacle of titanic objects and mechanisms. The viewers move slowly through this titanic laboroid space, amazed how all this could have been produced by their own hands. How these striking exaltations of steel and soil were shaped and mastered by their laboring hands.

It is here that the laborer gains historic justification and continues to toil away even more frenziedly.

VDNH is a cosmic laboroid monolith. The central pavilion houses the aircraft. The viewer, walking further in, reaches a huge circular space with a vast dome above it displaying a photograph of Gagarin: the first astronaut. Here the monolith opens its vault—the cosmos. The visitor finds his/her ultimate representative—the astronaut; and labor, its ultimate product—the spacecraft. On either side of VDNKh are placed Hotel Cosmos and the Monument of Space Exploration.

The cosmos is reassembled by hammer and sickle. Earth is cast in Heavens by a colossal laboroid hand.

## The Rambling Space: Arbat

*Perestroika* made possible the promiscuous space of Arbat Street. The political, religious, fictional spaces are of equal rights here in terms of street rambling. Orators, demonstrators, poets, Buddhists, prophets, astrologists, graphologists, magicians and loafers promiscuously segment the space of the street. There is no center here. No hierarchy of bodies, no strict demarcation between watching and acting. Space transfigures instantly.

The principle of constellations is the opposite of the collage principle, and the principle of the colossal monolith. Each and every moment an erotic will for life demonstrates at different corners of this street through different social masks. The daily rhythm of Moscow slows down and turns aimless along this street. The city knows no other place like this. Everywhere else it is organized in such a way that it makes the citizens purposeful marching body-machines. Here it dissipates so that the bodies turn to rambling.

The promiscuous codification of this street infects the bodies with Eros. A free human procession flows unrepressed by colossi and mummies.

## THE WITHERED STATE

In the draft program of the proletarian party Lenin presented the overthrow of the old system and its institutions in the following way: the founding of all-soviet militia and merging it with the army; all men and women aged 15 to 65 must participate in this militia on a mass scale.

This mass all-soviet participation in the army is presented as one of the forms of the withering away of the socialist state. The "proletarian dictatorship" does away with the old bourgeois state machine as it mobilizes the working people into mass all-soviet participation in all forms of social life. This represents the transitional stage when the state begins to wither away. The old state is disbanded while the new state withers away following its theoretical justification (see Lenin's *The State and Revolution*). The institutions, instruments and vehicles of the old state become all-soviet: private property, the army, the militia, the bureaucracy. The people itself becomes the soldier, the policeman and the clerk of the withered state.

The all-soviet collective body is the particular agent of the new state. The final aim is: a socially homogeneous and physically consolidated people plus sheer Party power. The Party, the master of the extra-state power, becomes all-soviet, which is a form of its withering as something particular, separate and superimposed. What has to remain is the Party-minded people consolidated as an homogeneous body and a uniform consciousness mobilized by the Party ideology.

The proletarian state has done nothing but to feign withering while it has never completely emerged from the body of the Party itself. In case of categorical establishment of a state system or of its complete withering, the Party power will become either something limited or something that lacks institutional enforcement.

The Party power is utterly maximized when the state is in a condition of permanent withering away. Party power is omnipotent when the people serve as soldier, policeman, clerk and owner of the state. It is precisely this merger between the people, the state and the Party, this radical growing together of the institutions and the public bodies, that makes Party power undefeatable.

The state chronically withers, merging with the Party body.


## THE EVERLASTING BODY-STEM OF COMMUNISM

*When Gregor Samsa woke up one morning . . .*
*he found himself changed in his bed into a monstrous*
*vermin*

                                   *Kafka*

Lenin died on 21 January 1924. On 26 January, the mourning conference of the Second Congress of the Soviets was opened, where Stalin made a speech. In it, on behalf of the Party, he pledged six oaths. The speech began with the following words: "We, the communists, are people of a special make. We are made of a special material."

Later on in the speech a recurring refrain appeared which interrupted the speech six times. In this refrain Lenin's six legacies were mentioned, followed by Stalin's six oaths. The refrain read as follows: "On leaving us, comrade Lenin bequeathed . . . We pledge to fulfill your bequest, comrade Lenin!"

The repetition "On leaving us, comrade Lenin . . . " is puzzling. In fact Lenin went nowhere because on 27 January, on the day following the oaths, he was laid in the Mausoleum. Thus he remained forever bequeathing to us and Stalin remained forever pledging to build and expand the Party space. Lenin could not leave because his body became the primal Party nucleus of power. It remained to stake out the territory where Stalin's Party imperialism was to expand.

Six days, from the 21st to the 27th, Lenin's body was laid out between the bed and the grave. Six times Stalin termed this body "leaving."

Stalin's speech began with the following words: "We, the communists, are people of a special make. We are made of a special material." The communist body does not decay!

The Mummy is the greatest communist. The stem of the Party.

The Mausoleum is the Center-accumulator mastering the collectivized people's libido.

The Mummy-stem in the Mausoleum-laboratory—this is the grand installation of modern political art and science.

### INDURATIO SPATII

The maximum of power is manifested as a Mummy stuck between life and death

The maximum of power is exposed as a stuffed centauric creature.

The communist centaur is out of joint!

The "inflammatory literature" to which this text belongs is a deliberately invented genre. It is a demonstrative, provocative manifestation of language aiming at two things in the least: First, to bring to an end the humble sterility of the theorizing language and its soft amorphous dimension choked with angered or dreamy metaphors. Language should inflame reality in order to expose the hidden foci of future cataclysms and decline. Second, to excite the imagination, to exult it and thus exorcise with language the brutal images, the aesthetic terrorists which have so far repressed our minds.

The Mummy is the greatest terrorist.

*Tell me frankly, what ought to remain of Lenin?*
*A. Rodchenko*

## Appendix: The Mummacrum of Power

### CONSOLIDATION OF THE MUMMY

#### Period 1

On 21 January 1924 Party membership card N 224332 became vacant forever. Thousands of cables and letters poured into the Central Committee. "Ilich," the workers insisted, "should physically remain with us in order to be seen by the vast working masses." "Do not commit his body to the earth! Embalm it and expose it at the Central museum!"

Soviet science was given the task to preserve the Leader's body for the longest time possible under the explicit condition that the features of his face should remain unchanged. Science responded as follows: It is difficult to predict the durability of the conservation. We can, however, guarantee it for two or three years.

The laboratories began intensive research work. A tomb for the Leader was built in the form of a

### CONSOLIDATION OF POWER

#### Period 1

Power is in a state of crisis.

The rivalry between Trotsky and Stalin is aggravated. Stalin pledges to fulfill Lenin's testament to consolidate the proletarian dictatorship.

An inert majority of proletarians is forced into the Central Committee according to Lenin's "Letter to the Congress" instructing how power is to be consolidated. Stalin conjures up Lenin's body with the words: "We, the communists are people of a special make, we are made of a special material."

public platform for speeches to be delivered to future generations. The constant observations of the embalmed body gave science rich experience and data. The same year the first mausoleum was erected hammered together out of planks and nails. Worshippers started lining up. *Pravda* wrote: "There he lays before their very eyes the same beloved Ilich clenching his right fist as if he is just about to rise and bang on the table."

## Half Period

Years passed. The painful parting with Lenin went on and on.

The confidence in the absolute success of the mummification was increasing from year to year. The chief mummificator Vorobev remembers one anxious night after long hours of work at the body when he noticed that the features of the face had started to change. Panic-stricken he woke up Dzerzhinskii to report. Fortunately science took the situation under control.

In 1929–30 it was already possible to speak of longer periods of conservation.

A decree was issued for the construction of a permanent mausoleum made out of granite.

## Period 2

In 1934 (the tenth anniversary of Lenin's death) a committee of

## Half Period

In 1929 Trotsky is exiled because of anti-Soviet and anti-socialist activities. In November Bukharin is expelled from the Politbureau.

Right-wing opportunists are condemned.

Mass repression.
Forced collectivization.

## Period 2

Stalin has liquidated all opposition in the party.

experts in charge of mummy-condition-monitoring concluded: "Lenin's body will be conserved for an indefinite time (i.e., forever)."

Worshippers were welcomed into a new red and black mausoleum—a unique achievement of the Soviet genius of construction.

The committee concluded that Lenin's mummification is an amazing feat of science with no precedent in history. Lenin's mummification won Professor Vorobev the Order of Lenin.

The Congress of Victors (the 17th Party Congress) declares the final victory of socialism. The delegates at this congress will not stay alive much longer.

Kirov, the main rival of Stalin, is murdered in December.

Mass terror strikes the Party itself.

## Half Period

1941–45. The mummy is evacuated. The existence of Ilich is in danger. A thorough inspection after the victory shows that transportation has fortunately done no harm.

The Soviet method of mummification has withstood all the ordeals of time.

A government committee declares that Ilich is preserved the way the people remember him. In 1949 the leader and the teacher of the Bulgarian comrades Georgi Dimitrov went to Moscow for medical treatment and was sent back to his liberated fatherland mummified through the Soviet method.

## Half Period

The Nazis reach Moscow. Soviet Power is at stake.

The USSR not only survives but manages to liberate other peoples, who are pushed along the path of socialism.

In 1949 Traitcho Kostov, a potential leader and teacher of the Bulgarian people, is tried and executed by the Soviet method.

## Period 3

After 1953 the Mausoleum was occupied for a while by Stalin's mummy lined up side by side with Lenin's. Later on, the former was buried behind the Mausoleum. (As rumor has it, it is still resisting decay because of its unique biochemical treatment.)

## Period 4

In 1964 high-tech electronic equipment was installed in the Mausoleum, to keep the temperature and humidity constant.

There is no end to the line of worshippers. Keeping in mind that each one is allowed an 80 second vigil, it would take 10,147 years for the entire human race to bid farewell to Ilich (presuming no one else is ever born).

After 1984 some say that Lenin should be buried according to the alleged hints he made in his last days.

P.S. In 1990 after extensive demonstrations the mausoleum in Sofia was assaulted.

The Dimitrov-mummy is secretly removed through underground passages and solemnly given last honors and buried.

## Period 3

Thaw; rejection of Stalinist "norms and principles"; return to Leninist "norms and principles."

## Period 4

A plenum of the Central Committee in 1964 retires Khrushchov and elects Brezhnev as General Secretary of the Party.

Stagnation begins. International consolidation of socialism.

Chernenko is sick.

Perestroika.

P.S. In 1990 power disintegrates with free elections.

As we can see the Body/Power (Soviet) Union followed a sixty-year cycle divided into four sub-cycles, namely; 10-20-10-20 years.

1924–1934 (consolidation)
1934–1954 (fortification)
1954–1964 (mollification)
1964–1984 (amplification) After 1984 the cycle is winding to an
end.

(Sources: *Mavzolei Lenina* [Moscow, 1946, 1972])

# 4

## Permutatio Publica

# The Birth of the Mummy from the Spirit of Ideology

The task of this section is to trace the process begun in Russia at the turn of the century which led to a translation of the concept of ideology from the Western critical tradition to the language of the Eastern revolutionary endeavor, a translation which entirely converted its axiological sign. We will confine our investigation to the shift in the understanding and conceptualization of ideology accomplished in the radical theoretical context built by the well-known scholarly circle of Bakhtin, Medvedev and Voloshinov. We hope the reader will find this retracing of the Eastern cycle of ideology provoking, though it may appear incommensurate with current Western intuitions. From a Western perspective the "progress" of ideology through the so-called Marxist-Leninist doctrine established in the 1920s in Soviet Russia may appear as an extreme deviation, a sharp veering off in a different direction. Yet, from an Eastern perspective, Leninism is the only forthright connection between Marx and the implementation of communism.

In what follows we will use the term *communism* mostly as the name of an ideological entity that kept its identity and secondary effects constant and immutable, in spite of changes in the power machinery, of economic reforms, or of any efforts to reconstruct or amend the system. We understand ideology as a strategically organized and self-authorized consciousness that builds a doctrine and designs tools for its implementation. It is precisely the main structure and key metaphors of this consciousness that we consider to be the intransitive core of communism. Now, let us go back to the radical times of the Revolution.

## The Axiom of Ideology

The state of the Soviets, in the 1920s—this is the place and the time when ideology merged with the real. The real was claimed to be a materialized ideology. At that time four books appeared written by three famous authors belonging to the same intellectual circle. Bakhtin is the actual author of one of them and the putative author of several other books written by this circle. We will not investigate the controversy concerning the authorship of these books, nor will we contribute to the ongoing debate on this issue. For our purposes, this controversy is irrelevant, because we regard the authorship as an ideological configuration, not a natural condition. The books of the Bakhtin circle built collectively a new context and strategy for the Soviet critical endeavor.

150

They speculated on the principle of ideology in its various forms—from its macropolitics to the microstructures of everyday life. The four books elaborated on a crucial issue at that time—ideology viewed as interest realized through the sphere of consciousness. The four books reflected on the ideologies of three major forms of life—fiction, language, psyche:

1.   The protagonist in Dostoevskii's fiction is an ideologist obsessed with an idée fixe who plots against other ideologists in order to realize and enforce it. This was Bakhtin's argument in *Problems of Dostoevskii's Poetics.*

2.   Language is an ideological phenomenon, it is a system of strategically organized sign-units. The sign is a meaningful unit that makes a dominant interest manifest. Reality is a set of meaningful units and must be recognized as a total ideological entity—this was Voloshinov's argument in *Marxism and the Philosophy of Language.*

3.   Bourgeois public life and the bourgeois moral surface of consciousness disguise rather than reveal the existence of a subliminal desire, interest or drive in social life. Every verbal act (utterance) is a small ideological construction which demonstrates the actual relation between the official and unofficial level of everyday consciousness—this is what Voloshinov argued in *Freudianism.*

Ideology testifies to the existence of something invisible—a basic interest which is economically generated, figuratively staged or disguised by morality. Ideology is a linguistic symptom of the basic interest. It makes the interest present in the sphere of consciousness.

4.   Ideology exists entirely in the external world and, by its origin, it is completely accessible to an essentially objective method of cognition. Human consciousness does not come into contact with existence directly but through the medium of the present ideological world. The ideological environment is materialized social consciousness. The work of art is a part of the materialized ideological horizon that surrounds man. Social beings are posed among ideological phenomena (words and objects). Ideology in its totality forms a solid ring around man—this is what Medvedev argued in *The Formal Method.*

We will focus more closely on one of these works because it is precisely this work which performed the radical shift in the concept of ideology that is the object of our investigation: the work is Voloshinov's *Marxism and the Philosophy of Language.* This book starts as radically as a manifesto would. Three propositions are important for our analysis: (1) The sphere of ideology coincides with the sphere of signs; (2) the word is an ideological phenomenon par excellence; and (3) ideology cannot be divorced from the material reality of the sign.

Voloshinov's book begins with axiomatic statements. It is significant and symptomatic that the focal term "ideology" is not elaborated theoretically. Ideology was a self-evident metaphor at that time, proliferating over the entire verbal territory of the Russian Revolution. It was borrowed from the realm of Party literature and the press, from the radical discourse of political manifestos, from the rhetoric of the grand political debate that was going on at that time. "Ideology" was a self-explanatory term taken from the agit-prop arsenal of revolutionary language.

Voloshinov's book openly claims that it represents the first general attempt to establish a Marxist philosophy of language. It keeps inviolate the main concepts of Marxist teaching but not the basic one—the axiological significance of "ideology." According to Marx, ideology was *twisted, incorrect, untrue—a false consciousness* alienated from the process of social reproduction and its foundations. Ideology was a pernicious consciousness, in Marx's view. But the use of the word "ideology" in Voloshinov's book has definitely a positive implication. This indicates that a certain revision, a reversal of meaning, had taken place in the meantime. Precisely this revision is the basic object of our investigation. The axiological shift was accomplished by Lenin. He related ideology to the campaigns of political power and defined ideology not as a "false consciousness" but as a "strategic" one aiming at a certain social end.

## THE HANGING GARDENS OF CONSCIOUSNESS

*The real world . . . has always been the apparent world
once again.*
       *Nietzsche,* The Will to Power, *no. 566*

### MARX: ALIENATION AND FALSIFICATION

*. . . ideology is a process accomplished by the thinker
consciously, indeed, but with a false consciousness. The
real motives impelling him remain unknown to him,
otherwise it would not be an ideological process at all.*
       *Engels (Seliger 1977, 30)*

In the theories of Marx and Engels ideology is critiqued as a *false consciousness* which comes to reinforce the dominant illusion of society. Such ideology is speculative philosophy, the queen of fabrications. According to Marx, ideology screens the real struggle of antagonistic interests, enacting a visionary topos of social and political oblivion, where the real constitution of life is replaced by a replica. Ideology manufactures ersatz interests.

Metaphysics was blamed by Marx for having glorified the detached, immovable mind for centuries. The thinking subject was blamed for being noninvolved in the immediate bustle of social life. Philosophy was attacked for actually suspending the mind by assigning to it artificial logical ends, fragile moral props and elusive foundations. Ideology is a false consciousness made discursive which has captured minds and has authorized and institutionalized its own phantom-like products. It is a manufacturing system of illusions and prejudices that blocks the efforts of sound reason to get to the real source of life.

### FREUD: THE SHATTERED SUR-FACE OF THE PSYCHE

Freud's critique does something similar. It terms "secondary-process thinking," or "secondary elaboration" a false representation which conceals the subliminal conflicts of the psyche. Consciousness fabricates the official façade of desire and makes it publicly appropriate. The *psyche* is regarded as a twisted mirror of sexual endeavors that are ruled by the economy of libido. Consciousness is the sur-face of psyche whereupon the figures of its lower depth are engraved. If you do not know how to read the figures of consciousness and thus to expose the depths of the psyche, you will be confined to the world of surface appearances masquerading as genuine. According to Freud, consciousness censors and screens the obnoxious urges of the psyche, thus making it comply with the public habit. In spite of its faults, it is precisely consciousness which is nominated as the great physician who reads the ciphers of life, gives the diagnosis and carries out the treatment. Both Marx and Freud counted on the analytical capabilities of consciousness to provide a healthy critique. Marx and Freud launched several critiques against "false consciousness" by exposing the deceiving mechanism that masks the sur-face of life. Ideology is a suggestive epi-phenomenal complex of visions and motivations which enciphers in itself the real foundation of life. They have to be deciphered and thus dispelled.

Ideology is a grand fabrication. Its stages are alienation of the consciousness from the reproductive principle of social life, and reification of its false products as true values of life, blocking the access of reason to the real source—the basic interest. Ideology can be dethroned either by revolutionary action or through a scientific critique and (psycho)analytical procedures. The critical mode of reason is a clinic for the ideologically spoiled consciousness.

## NIETZSCHE: THE VALUE SYSTEM
## AS A STRATEGIC FABRICATION

*"Truth": this, according to my way of thinking, does
not necessarily denote the antithesis of error, but in the
most fundamental cases only the posture of various errors in relation to one another.*
Nietzsche, The Will to Power, *no. 535*

Nietzsche's critical approach was more radical. According to him, the very constitution of consciousness makes it falsify. Consciousness is the most vehement agent of the will to vision (*der Wille zum Schein*). It incites the initial vision of the "as if" world (*als ob*).

Nietzsche was drawn to a radical critique of values. Values are nuclei that generate the motivations of life and that have accumulated huge power. They are fortified and guarded by different historically changing sets of metaphors, symbolic devices and social disciplines. Values minister the flux of life and endow it with a ceremonial fashion. The ministry of values represses life as an end in itself. Values, those victorious prejudices and representations of good and evil, false and true, confine the ecstatic source of life. Values are not the intrinsic matter and eternal essence of life. A value is a sheer instruction that disciplines the original impulse of the mind and body. It is only later in the course of history that values acquire the status of being the essence of life. People forget that values were initially metaphors built into the living tissue of society. Values are fabrications charged with maximum power and thus made real. The value system is a metaphorical composition, resting on imagined figures that have been taken out of their original poetic order and later installed in the world as a doctrine. Morals are poesis transformed into doctrine.

At the source of every system of values is *der Wille zum Schein*. The transformation of this will's product (*das Scheinbild*) into a doctrine, determines it as "will to power." The generative voluntarism that composes and empowers the value system puts the will into a position of absolute authority. It constantly returns to its ecstatic source, recovers as an artful forger of *Scheinbilds* and invents new unprecedented figures and metaphors, building thus a new value doctrine or repairing an old one.

### ENTER LENIN

For Marx, Nietzsche and Freud everything revolved around a major social and psychological resource agitated by the desire to increase—

*capital, will to power, libido.* For Freud and Marx ideology obscured the basic social or psychological interest through the sphere of consciousness. Conversely, Nietzsche considered any endeavor of the consciousness a strategic falsification which does not cover up but rather stimulates the reproduction of the resource and reinforces the basic interest. The common formula is: consciousness plus power equals ideology. A bold consciousness forges ideologies through which a particular drive, stimulation or excitement rushes in to take over life.

The ideological mode of consciousness is composed of values (Nietzsche), of speculations (Marx) and of misleading elaborations (Freud). Hence, it was the goal of consciousness to abolish its metaphysical fabrications, to destroy the detrimental idols, fetishes and simulacra it has forged in the course of history, and to return to the vital source of life. Thus the original integrity between the principle of consciousness and the reproductive principle of life must be restored. Before Lenin ideology was treated as a deviation of consciousness, something that could be overcome by the critical faculties of consciousness itself.

Then Lenin entered the stage. He easily corrected Marx's concept of ideology (false consciousness), because he, like Nietzsche, posed the issue through the perspective of power. Lenin considered ideology as a strategic claim to power. Ideology was defined by him as a major weapon in the struggle for power and a major vehicle for reinforcing power. The end of ideology is in its final reification a power system.

IDEOLOGY: CONSCIOUSNESS FROM WITHOUT

*We said that there could not yet be Social-Democratic consciousness among the workers. This consciousness could only be brought to them from without. . . . the working class, exclusively by its own effort, is able to develop only trade union consciousness. . . . The theory of socialism, however, grew out of the philosophic, historical and economic theories that were elaborated by the educated representatives of the propertied classes, the intellectuals. According to their social status, the founders of modern scientific socialism, Marx and Engels, themselves belonged to the bourgeois intelligentsia.*
Lenin, "What is to be Done," p. 74

*Modern socialist consciousness can arise only on the basis of profound scientific knowledge. . . . Thus socialist consciousness is something introduced into the proletarian class struggle from without, and not something that*

*arose within it spontaneously. Accordingly . . . the task*
*of Socialist-Democracy is to imbue the proletariat with*
*the consciousness of its position and the consciousness*
*of its tasks.*
Karl Kautsky *(Lenin, "What is to be Done," p. 81–82)*

In his famous book "What is to be Done" (1902) Lenin formulates the essence of proletarian ideology as opposed to the bourgeois one, representing the most developed form of class struggle. The fundamental concept there is the double genealogy of the proletarian momentum: the genealogy of the class-unconscious impulse for economic struggle and the genealogy of the class-self-consciousness highly organized in proletarian ideology.

The impulse arose in the laboring masses and the ideology was developed by the intellectuals who belonged to the bourgeois milieu. Lenin makes clear that the "spontaneous" and the "conscious" elements of the movement originate independently. Nevertheless they complete each other on the stage of the class struggle. These two elements conjugate and create perfect revolutionary vanguards and their difference withers away. The proletarian movement finds its final integrity when reaching this highest organizational stage.

The impulse (spontaneity) arises within the union of the toiling masses. Democratic intelligentsia elaborates the proletarian proper ideology and introduces it to the workers from without their union. The intelligentsia is charged with the mission to imbue proletarian endeavor with strategic consciousness and to keep raising it through agitation and propaganda. Originally the social body of the ideologist did not belong to the class union. The mind of the ideologist was not involved in the spontaneous campaigns of the toiling masses. The ideologist stands detached while brooding over the total picture of ideology and realizing the political purpose of the class interest. There are two awakenings of the movement: one for strikes (economic claims) and the other for revolution (political claims). Workers by themselves can only reach up to the level of trade-unionism. Then, from without penetrates the ideology worked out in a detached scientific contemplation to mobilize them for revolution and to structure their interest into a party.

There are two strategies of the class struggle: legal, which posits particular trade-union claims and underground, which posits the political claim for total empowerment of proletarians. The legal way could turn misleading because it could engage the class exclusively in activities complying with the bourgeois legal and moral system, thus the movement diverts to opportunism. There is one way to prevent this: to subordinate the legal activities to the ultimate political objective (the building of a new proletarian society) and the ultimate political means (the revolution.) Lenin's postulate is clear: the legal organizations of workers and their activities should be completely subordinated to the underground momentum of the movement and its conspiratorial campaigns. The labor movement engaged exclusively in legal activities could divert and give in completely to the bourgeois ideology and value system. The spontaneous claim for rights can be fashioned in accord to the bourgeois consciousness and political system. Thus the movement can be imbued by a false consciousness, made embrace false objectives and pursue a false cause. Lenin stressed the exclusive mission and responsibility of the professional revolutionary who has to carry out an immense conspiratorial work in order to prevent any bourgeois diversion in the movement by impregnating it with sound elements and sound, proletarian-proper ideology, conducting a mass scale instruction.

The party purposeful activism sublimates the unconscious proletarian spontaneity channeling it through the system of party ideology and organizations. This prevents the originally pure proletarian impulse from bourgeois corruption. The revolutionary cause keeps the impulse sound and vigilant.

Ideology unites impulse and consciousness. Thus it triggers revolution.

Since there can be no talk of an independent ideology being developed by the masses of the workers in the process of their movement the only choice is: either bourgeois or socialist ideology. There is no middle course for humanity has not created a "third" ideology . . .
*Lenin, "What is to be Done," p. 82*

For Lenin there were two antagonist ideologies (*tertium non datur*), revolutionary and bourgeois, party activism and reaction. Revolutionary ideology challenges the bourgeois world as a whole, its superstructure, its super-ego, its false consciousness and will to power which had all proved to be completely wrong to provide the legal motive and moral code for the vehemently emerging proletarian impulse. Armed with a counter-ideology the party activism develops the underground in order to undermine and finally demolish the whole oppressive bourgeois system. This underground and its conspiratorial campaigns open a whole alternative space for raising correct consciousness that will direct and fully gratify the storming proletarian impulse. Only the underground can raise a politically correct proletarian consciousness.

Party conspiracy and discipline form revolutionary-proper super-structure and enforce revolutionary-proper super-ego to master the unconscious proletarian impulse, spontaneity and vigor.

Party conspiracy is the one form that radically merges impulse and ideology, toiling body and strategic consciousness, worker and intellectual. Conspiratorial work creates a new ideal man—the professional revolutionary—a tough body and sharp mind coated in suggestive incognito that utterly propagates revolution and agitates the masses to storm the old world.

### WHAT IS IDEOLOGY?

Ideology is a deliberately created system of visions and "bold metaphors" aimed at defeating or promoting the basic interest. At this point we need to distinguish between a *false consciousness* and a *falsifying consciousness*. In both cases ideology is considered to be the major vehicle for the basic interests which strive to penetrate the realm of official power.

Ideology appears when a strategic will or interest penetrates and impregnates consciousness. It launches a consciousness-raising campaign and instructs consciousness to claim power. The power-granted consciousness implements its projects into reality.

Ideology comes to demonstrate and empower a strategic human faculty that has been traumatized by rigid politics and morals. It comes to enable an arrested development, to replace the sclerotic vessels and conductors of the will and to fortify the world with new metaphors and symbolic devices. Ideology puts together a world of appearance (*Schein*) by manufacturing and assembling "bold metaphors." Ideology is a constellation of visions which comes to enforce or to defeat a particular endeavor. The source of this strategic fabrication is the will to power, capital, or the libido.

A structure built of metaphors (appearances) and loaded with maximum resources acquires the status of a value/power doctrine. Any doctrine puts forth a system of values and completely obliterates the traces of its arbitrary artistic origin. The victorious implementation of "bold metaphors" and visions depends on the amount of power invested in them. The communist doctrine ultimately consolidated "the will to power" in a Party, "the will to vision" in a Teaching, the capital in a grand construction of industrial visions, the libido in a sublime communal jubilation and superhuman feats of labor.

### TENTATIVE CONCLUSIONS

1.  Ideology neither can be verified, nor falsified. Ideology cannot be true or false for it creates by itself what justifies it. Hence it is either "sound" or "sick."

2.  Ideology is a self-propelled device. The operative principle is
    the following: the device itself creates the jet that propels it.
    This is the operative principle of the rocket in outer space. The
    ship itself creates the sea it sails. Ideology, as a self-sufficient
    and self-propelled entity, can act in a void.

## IDEOLOGY AND SIGNIFICATION

*Any ideological product is not only itself part of a real-
ity (natural or social) just as is any physical body, any
instrument of production or any product for consumption; in contradistinction to the latter, it also reflects
and refracts another reality lying outside itself. Everything ideological possesses meaning: it represents, depicts, or stands for something lying outside itself, i.e., it
is a sign. Where there is no sign, there is no ideology.*
*Voloshinov (1930, 13)*

Lenin's concern was how to reorganize the sphere of consciousness so
that it might start generating proper proletarian images that directly
manifested the labor-force interest. Communist ideology externalized
the interest it stood for, objectifying it directly in the public space. This
ideology became the proper vehicle the Party interest operated by, man
ifesting immediately its availability and claims. The crown was replaced by the cogwheel; hammer and sickle replaced the bow and
arrow. The very means of production and manufacturing goods, which
the workers had been alienated from, now became the emblems of the
nonalienated class consciousness of communism.

Leninism is the ideology of a Revolution. From its perspective, ideology is a strategically organized consciousness claiming to express and represent completely the basic class interest, that of the labor force. Revolutionary ideology mobilizes this interest through the sphere of consciousness. Revolutionary ideology does not disguise but, on the contrary,
articulates the interest. According to Lenin, revolutionary ideology is not
an alienated consciousness; quite the contrary, it is a politically imposed interest through the vehicles of consciousness. The Red Party represents the
supreme stage of a strategically organized class consciousness. The Party
is the final achievement of the political self-consciousness of the working
class. The Party is the political vanguard of the proletariat. It implements
class interest straight into power. Only in this way can the *suppressed class
consciousness* of the workers become *official*, that is, unsuppressed.

By seizing political power, class interest, the class self-consciousness
and the superorganized Party ideology grew into a national interest, national consciousness and national ideology. Communist power emerged

as the supreme stage of class consciousness. After the Revolution, the official sphere of power and the sphere of consciousness coincided and this marked the end of Red ideology.

Nadezhda Krupskaia states: "There is no doubt that the ideology of the proletariat is different from the ideology of the other classes. . . . Each class has its own ideology. . . . The concept of ideology includes also morality, art and science. Nobody would deny that the bourgeois morality radically differs from the proletarian one" (1980, 122).

Following the description quoted above, a distinction between revolutionary and reactionary ideology emerges. The clue that differentiates them is the following: the ideology which disguises the class interest it virtually represents is a reactionary one. The ideology which frames the basic interest, handles it and directs it towards a final victory of the working class is a revolutionary one.

Communism continually changed its ideological course, the key metaphors and names, with the single purpose of staying in power by generating ever-changing knowledge for the system. There was in fact a permanent usurpation of power by new words. Every single moment communist power was reconfirmed through newer and newer names: at one time to modernize society, at another to smash the enemy, at another still to collectivize the population, then to expose the conspiracy of the traitors, later to build the first "stage of socialism," then to build another stage that denied the previous one, then to revise the way and the means, then to change the leader, and so on. Somewhere in the conspiratorial spaces of Party power the ideology was worked out together with the plot for the next seizure of power. A new Party plenum comes, the course is changed, a new ideological strategy is formulated, the worn-out metaphors are replaced by recently fabricated ones. Communism is in action.

The political dimension of ideology and its Party emanation are its most suggestive forms.

**THE ODYSSEUS EFFECT:**

**THE CONSTANT RETURN OF THE AUTOCRAT TO POWER**

Lenin's problem was to develop the Marxist Teaching into an ideology according to which to construct a new world and establish a power of justice in it. Stalin's problem was to constantly improve ideology and thus keep holding power in his hands as the next author of the Teaching. Stalin had the chronic urge to repeat constantly the take-over of the power he already held. The delirious economy of his consciousness mass-produced enemies and phantom-like rivals. That made Stalin per-

manently reinstate his power and through terror disperse his own
ghostly apparitions.

Stalin, like Odysseus, was in a state of everlasting return to Ithaca,
permanently ready to exterminate the bridegrooms hanging about the
powerful object of his desire—the bride who awaits her mate, weaving
the sheet of their expected reunion. Stalin was never in power. He was
returning to power all the time and constantly trying to disperse his
paranoid visions of the competing "bridegrooms." At night he used to
wander in his underwear, gun in hand, through the silent corridors of
the Kremlin. Returning from the distant worlds of his own nightmares,
he was ready to shoot all the "grooms" hiding in the dark.

The fact that the will to vision (der Wille zum Schein) degenerates
from ideology into paranoia, is a symptom of the increasing inability
of the ideologist to survive in "this" system of power. Totalitarian
power marks the merger of a super-generative ideology and a super-
degenerative paranoia. Political paranoia is a historical de-generation
of ideology. The repressed one is a historically degenerate revolutionary. Fear is a historically degenerate form of self-denial. What made you
initially plunge bright-eyed into the battle for the future, later forces you
to step back dull-eyed in panic.

The bright idea returns as a monstrous body. This historical eclipse
or menopause of power coincides with the moment when grand ideol
ogy turns into an everyday world and visions turn into bodies. This is
the moment when communism actually wins.

### THE PLOT OF THE REVOLUTIONARY UNCONSCIOUS

*Not every motive that confronts the official ideology de-
generates and dies in the turbulence of inner speech—it
may also initiate a struggle against the official ideology.
Such a motive, if it stems from the economic definitions
of a whole group, and if it is not the motive of an isolated social degenerate, may have a social future and
probably a victorious one. . . . In the beginning this motive develops in a small social area, then it goes underground, not in the psychic underground of displaced
complexes, but in the sound political underground. And
precisely thus a revolutionary ideology originates in all
spheres of culture.*

Voloshinov (1983)

Freud actually preached on behalf of the bourgeois superego; this is the
general accusation levied against him by Voloshinov, who follows the

Marxist perspective in criticism. The aim of his book *Freudianism,* is to correct the Freudian scheme and to prove that the plot of the unofficial working class consciousness may have a healing effect if it succeeds in replacing the old bourgeois superego with a historically progressive one. Voloshinov accomplished a radical reversal. He transferred the issue of ideas from the sphere of the psyche into the sphere of the political struggle for power. In this way he replaced the opposition between the conscious/unconscious levels of the psyche with that between the official/unofficial political endeavor of a class-determined consciousness which results in two ideological "complexes" claiming power. The *underground* ideology of the exploited class aims at removing the *official* one and replacing it by a new social organism and a new psyche. This is the only way the interest of the exploited can be legalized and not be considered criminal anymore. Instead of being subjected to psychoanalysis, the repressed and exploited life-forces of the proletarian psyche must join the politically organized underground, must be channeled into a political conspiracy, exhausting themselves completely in a revolutionary movement, whose main object is to expose and to dethrone (castrate) the bourgeois *superego.* Revolution justifies the illegal character of the underground class forces, providing them with a political formula.

Voloshinov's alternative program was explicitly articulated: in lieu of becoming sick, in lieu of suffering psychic disturbances, one had to join the conspiratorial underground movement. For Revolution was a grand psychoanalytical session wherein the physician (the Party) led the exploited out of the social unconscious which imposed itself as the new superego. The alienated proletarianized social body generated its anti-official, underground ideological "complex," which represented its immediate economic interest and claims to power. Its jagged cutting edge became the Communist Party, the utterly organized proletarian self-consciousness.

The Red Party organized itself and acted in a perfect conspiracy, which was the ultimate manifestation of the underground class interest. This obtained on one side of the front a proletarian body dissociated from the social organism with a completely developed underground class consciousness represented by its conspiratorially acting vanguard; and on other side, the bourgeois ideological machine assembled by the repressive organs of the state, religious code and morals, philosophy and a social science which falsified the true situation in the social depths.

### IDEOLOGY AS A RESOUNDING EXTERIOR

*The social psychology is present nowhere inside but entirely outside: in word, in gesture, in act. There does not*

*exist any unexpressed interior. Everything is visible,
everything is rendered in space, in material, but first
and foremost in the material of the word.*
                                          *Voloshinov (1930, 23)*

The semiotic system of the Revolution is a radically exteriorized revolutionary self-consciousness, or a consciousness made objectively present outside any subject.

Voloshinov and his com-peer Bakhtin argued that the principle of ideological togetherness of the collective life (*sobornost'*) is a dialogical one. In the process of the dialogue different individual consciousnesses get together but they do not run the dialogue. The dialogue performs through them.

Dialogue is a *polyphony* of sounding and resounding voices which share common existential terms (de-termination). The consciousness of the "other" faces "myself" as a voice. The voice represents the personal interior resounding in a body. The body becomes the tongue of the interior. Thus the interior is exteriorized in order to encounter the interior of the "other," which in turn resounds in the same way.

Dialogue enacts voices that break against each other. But the language which builds the dialogue is not proper to any voice. The linguistic means for the production of any social dialogue are present entirely outside any voice and any individual consciousness. They are present "in between," they terminate any consciousness from outside, they are materialized in different places without being proper to any particular place and any particular body. They are ideological systems of the sort Bakhtin sees in the works of Dostoevskii and in the world of Rabelaisean carnival culture. In Dostoevskii's works the voices stand for autonomous consciousness. In Rabelais, they stand for autonomous bodies. But there is a third position: that of Bakhtin, the author himself, that of the philosophizing consciousness. He uses a special term for it—*vne-nahodimost'*, that is, the outside-presence of the meditating consciousness. The philosophizing consciousness has its own foundation and does not share the definitions of the ideology it speculates on.

To sum up, the genuine tools of ideology, be they voices, signs, or linguistic devices, are always outside-present and have an extrapersonal origin.

The revolutionary semiotic system builds a resounding grand public exterior where voices are made to echo, bodies get disciplined, consciousness becomes organized.

The semiotic system of revolutionary agit-prop is the third one after Rabelais and Dostoevskii which Voloshinov and his tutor failed to present for us.

Agit-prop culture can be analyzed as ideology turned into a grand reverberating exterior.

**IDEOLOGY BANDAGES THE VOID:**

**THE EFFECT OF THE INVISIBLE MAN**

*Everything is visible, everything is rendered in space, in*
*physical material, but first and foremost in the material*
*of the word.*

*Voloshinov (1930, 23)*

You all know the story of the Invisible Man.

The invisible man wraps himself up in bandages in order to become visible. In fact he never becomes visible. Only bandages mark his presence in space. The invisible man wraps himself up in a visible material so as to make his transparent body distinct. Thus transparency becomes opaque, that is, visible. The specter acquires dense reality only in the outfits.

Communist ideology performed a manipulation of the same kind. It turned itself into the virtual body of the otherwise invisible communist world. Its words, images, figures and monumental packaging became the body of the bright world. This world appeared only as an ideological visionary complex.

Ideology wraps up no real world that either precedes or follows it. This was rather a world that strapped down people. When the Party doctrine was overthrown, the world of communism instantly disappeared. The strategic vision withered away and laid bare a wrecked reality. Ideology generated no real world but the effect of a world. It projected a world and the moment the source of projection was completely erased, the population found itself lined up staring at the void. The genuine realities of communism are the figures of the Teaching, the monumental space that staged it, the bandages of the slogans, the hard cover of the symbols and the communist emblems.

The wrecked ideology opens up holes through which monsters of reality peep.

**DETERMINATOR: THE ULTIMATE SIGN**

*Ideology can not be divorced from the material reality of*
*the sign.*

*Voloshinov (1930, 25)*

Communism produced a radical materialization of terror. The political unconscious of the masses was opened up and its figures released, exteriorized as a grand public space replete with macabre imagery, organized around the ultimate sign of the Party conspiratorial consciousness—the mummy Lenin—the Grand Determinator of reality.

Mummified Lenin is the ultimate ideological sign. Its unique outstanding presence (*vne-nahodimost*) is exposed in a sacred underground interior—a mausoleum. Lenin's body is intact and through embalming is eternalized and safeguarded against decomposition. It gathers the community together shaping it into two general forms: a mourning line and an exalting parade in front of its dwelling place.

The Mummy is the point at which pure class self-consciousness acquires corporality and reaches its virtual end. The virtual (corpo)reality appears when real and the visual coincide. Society is consolidated around the mummified carnal substance of the Leader's body. The ultimate sign is created of a special material and is an object of a special make. The ideology it testifies to can not be divorced from its substance.

The Mummy is the virtual end of communism.

Without a Mummy, communism has no

*— End.*

# Of the (Post-)Conspiratorial Society

## REVOLUTION AND CONSPIRACY:
## CODE AND ORGANIZATION

1.1   *The structure of the organization is based on individual trust.*

1.2   *The organizer (himself a member) selects five or six persons from amongst his acquaintances and, having held a separate discussion with and secured the consent of each, assembles them together and lays the foundation of a closed cell. . . .*

1.5   *A member of the organization immediately forms in his turn a second degree cell around himself, in relation to which the previously formed cell assumes the role of a central cell. . . .*

2.1   *The revolutionary is a dedicated man. He has no interests of his own, no affairs, no feelings, no attachments, no belongings, not even a name. . . .*

2.2   *In the very depths of his being . . . he has broken every tie with the civil order and the entire cultured world, with all its laws, proprieties, social conventions and its ethical rules. . . .*

2.4    *... For him, everything is moral which assists the triumph of revolution. ...*

2.13   *The revolutionary enters into the world of the state, of class and so-called culture, and lives in it only because he has faith in its speedy and total destruction. He is not a revolutionary if he feels pity for anything in this world. If he is able to, he must face the annihilation of a situation, of a relationship or of any person who is a part of this world—everything and everyone must be equally odious to him. ...*

2.14   *Aiming at merciless destruction the revolutionary can and sometimes even must live within society while pretending to be quite other than what he is. ...*

2.26   *To knit this world into a single invincible and all-destroying force—this is the purpose of our entire organization, our conspiracy, and our task.*

*Sergei Nechaev, "Catechism of the Revolutionist," 1869*
*(Sternberg and Bott 1974, 221–30)*

## The League of the Just

*In the year 1834 a group of German refugees in Paris founded a secret society known as the League of the Proscribed. ... During 1836 the most extreme, most proletarian elements broke away and constituted themselves into a new secret League of the Just. ... The new League, however, developed rather quickly. ... The aims of the Just were the same as those of the other Parisian secret societies of the period. The League was thus about equally divided between propaganda and conspiratorial work.*

*F. Engels (Struik 1971, 150)*

## The Conspiratorial Perspective of Communism

Communism could be regarded as the boldest conspiratorial action ever undertaken. It comprised two phases, an underground and a legal one, separated by the watershed of the Revolution, and followed by a peculiar post-conspiratorial condition of society. During each of its general conspiratorial campaigns communism changed the image and form of its public manifestations, as well as the substance of its opacity, its political disguise and symbolic codification.

### CONSPIRACY AS A SELF-SUFFICIENT SOCIETY

Communism is a political conspiracy based on strict rules and procedures of initiation, ritual communication, secret passwords, aliases and call-signs. A clear-cut ideology becomes the motor of the political confederacy charged with the impetus of a belief and assembled through the formulas of a "science." The ideology is expressed at the same time as a moral duty, as a pattern for rationalizing the world, and as an object of desire. It is the institution which provides the conspiracy with moral, rational and erotic motivation, and thereby provides the conspirator with strict socialization. Conspiratorial life is ostensibly ceremonial, fanatically amorous, heroically sacrificial, politically expedient, scientifically justified, ordered by its own extraordinary statutes, institutions and executive bodies. Conspiracy is a complete society which creates by itself the ideological justifications of its own being.

The conspiracy originates within "this" type of society with the mission to abolish it. It is in the frame of a legal type of society that conspiracy develops its political disguise and in this way builds itself up as the alternative social unity. The alternative society is present incognito within the legal terms of "this" society and that is the formula of revolutionary conspiracy.

### GENEALOGY

According to one rather popular view, the agents of any alternative social formation to come are born within the economic structures of the present one, where they organize new forms of economic relationships and interests that gradually become political, forming a politically representative body that undertakes a struggle for power so that it can represent the interests of a historically new economic subject. Similarly, the inception of the communist movement is attributed to the political vanguard of the proletariat: the Communist Party. But later on it turned out that communism takes power in countries with a weak proletariat, low concentration of capital and an obstructed political life.

After it came to power the Communist Party carried out a strategic industrialization in order to mass-produce its own social base—the working class—and it began a methodical extermination of the peasantry. For quite a long time the peasants were even denied the right to have identity cards which testifies that they were treated as illegitimate and nonrepresentative social agents from a communist perspective, as citizens of the former, already abolished society.

Inversely, countries where the working class was traditionally strong proved very resistant to communism. Communism proved to be a system of an extra-economic origin which cannot be rationalized in terms of capital and economically-structured societies. The "working class" of communism has no economic definition. Such a political determination of people who are aware of their common economic interest, unanimously agree on their goals and rally round a definite view simply does not exist. And where such a determination really exists, people get involved in a struggle against the political system called communism.

As a self-sufficient system, communism was born within the "old" society not as an economic but as a party conspiratorial agent. It imposes the interest of the Party underground militant. The organism of the Party was and remains conspiratorial and in this sense party-interest even on power is imposed through conspiratorial plots and techniques.

The Communist Party is not a bourgeois type of party that represents the particular economic interests of a guild or class. It is a conspiracy and in this sense its objective is not to get in the power administration but to usurp the entire power and replace its foundation. This is because the conspiracy is an integral secret society which takes over and expands throughout the entire social space.

## CONSPIRACY, PLOT, MACHINATION

A plot or a machination do not challenge the power system in which they were designed. They solve certain problems of the power system itself that cannot be solved in a lawful and overt way. In contrast, the revolutionary conspiracy challenges society as a whole: the state, public, class and economic structures. The plot and machination result in a public scandal. Conspiracy revolves the wheel of history.

## UNDERGROUND STAGE

The conspiracy creates the first masks of its political incognito in underground conditions. It develops its own secret language, a chain of conspiratorial names and metaphors borrowed from the Teaching. It erects its idols and truths charged with strong symbolic power, so that people may die for them. It replaces the proper names with aliases and creates an all-round incognito existence of its agents. It introduces an integral coded system of communications and government. It creates its own secret "police," "judiciary," and "press." It creates a whole "otherwise-functioning" space of secret meetings, hiding places, re-named sites and objects, coded topoi, and saturates this space with the magic words and gestures of the Teachers and Leaders.

The conspiracy symbolically impregnates space. Only those initiated in its cryptograms can move around in it.

### LEGAL STAGE

By means of its revolutionary campaign the Red conspiracy removed the society within which it originated but retained and later imposed its own definitions, turning them into the legal system of the new society. In this sense communism, as a conspiratorial society, cannot be built, it can only be officially inaugurated or superimposed.

The communist conspiracy appropriates the whole power through revolution. The revolution is the grand social action, the extra-moral and extra-legal origin of which has been made sacramental and pro-claimed inimitable through the Red ideology. Communism is justified in terms of the world and mankind to come.

### THE SIMULATION

The conspiracy seized the whole power and became legal. We make dif-ference between the concepts of *legal* and *legitimate*. Something is legal if it does not contradict the law and justifies its existence through the law. The law may not contain explicit provisions for the existence of any such particular phenomenon. For example, the law does not say whether a workers' party should or should not exist. It comes under the competence of the law only after such party has appeared by itself. On the other hand, a phenomenon is *legitimate* if: (1) It has been categori-cally enacted and regulated by the law. In this sense, Parliament is a le-gitimate division of power. A legitimate entity cannot be regarded as legal or illegal insofar as it is made by the law and does not depend on some one's will expressed in accordance with the law or in spite of the law. (2) Besides, legitimacy insists on the representative character of the political phenomena, delegated through a due legislative process. From this point of view the Communist Party by its conspiratorial principle may be "legal" if it does not break any existing law, but it is not legiti-mate as the only party in power, at least for two reasons: its Party lead-ership that has merged with the state power has been elected through Party vote and discipline rather than by general elections. Thus the Party imposes the interests of the conspiracy on the structures of the state. Moreover, its exclusive leading role is decreed by the Constitution. Its first article reads that the only party—the communist one—has the leading role in the socialist state and that the Communist Party is an all-national representative. That automatically undermines the very essence of a constitution as fundamental law of the state which ought to decree the possible forms of political life, not the specific entities involved in it. Legitimacy concerns the procedure of authorization. There is a difference between the legal existence and the legitimate power of a party.

Thus a party is legal if its existence dos not break the law, but its power is legitimate only if the party has been freely delegated certain prerogatives through a legal procedure and represents particular social interests and political will.

The legal, post-revolutionary phase of the conspiracy is characterized by a chronic illegitimacy of its absolute power. Consequently, the Party copes with its illegitimacy through symbolic means and conjuring words, exactly as it did when it was an underground agent. The conspiratorial society is ruled by symbols rather than law because it is based on symbols rather than economics. The conspiratorial state is not a juridical entity but rather an aesthetic outfit of the Party. The Party disguises its chronic illegitimacy by enacting an exclusive mission prior to any state constitution.

The conspiratorial society created effect of a state. The whole appearance of it is a grand simulacrum charged with an immense Party will to power and precisely for that reason experienced as real.

The simulation is a strategic effort to secure or usurp power.

The temporal paradox of the conspiratorial society consists in the fact that the past comprises a series of wrong initiatives, errors and distortions which methodically make the future recede into the distance. That is precisely what renders the current condition of society crucial and revolutionary. That perpetuates the condition of permanent revolution which, as was already mentioned, represents the extreme state of conspiracy.

By dissimulating statehood the Red conspiracy methodically distorts its own extra-state origin. Under this condition the most monstrous atrocities have occurred. The conspiracy forms a fake state and in terms of this state it begins to behave antisocially.

FASCISM/COMMUNISM

Totalitarian power organized in a conspiratorial way has nothing in common with fascist power. Fascism is an ideologically motivated and symbolically expressed social exultation which, however, is incited and mastered by a legitimate power and a party vision that has become a genuine national obsession. Fascism is not a conspiracy, has no split (legal/underground) existence and does not simulate statehood. In the case of fascism a merger has indeed occurred between the state and the party which resulted in a colossal political and economic effect: a rapid growth of industry, a high concentration of capital, a great consolidation of the working people round the body of power. In Germany the party doctrine of Nazism was nationally enforced through elections and legitimate procedures and then made itself into a state.

Communism came to power by means of a revolution, did away with the entire former society and established a tentative statehood for the purpose of making it eventually "whither away." Under communism there is no fusion of party and state but rather a manufactured appearance of statehood that screens the on-going party conspiracy.

Fascism has nothing in common with the political motive of communism and its public dissimulation. Nazi teaching is pernicious precisely because it positively decrees a nation as the only bearer of the genuine human nature. It is stripped down to the forms of a racial-organic aggression which has a positive biological description and eliminates anything which does not fit into it. Nazi dictatorship targets the "other" people and is realized through expansion. The manifestation of the *race-party strategy* differs radically from the manifestation of the *class-party strategy*. The former postulates the natural condition of the superior race and demands "sanitization" of humankind, while the latter endeavors to create an unprecedented political condition of the "class," applying symbolic manipulation and conjuration. The conspiracy experiments alchemy for class perfection; fascism—chemistry for race perfection.

Drawing of analogies between fascism and communism can have a moral effect but has a very low cognitive coefficient.

### CONSPIRACY AS A MORAL CASE

The "Western" perspective dispels conspiracy as social mode. In terms of Western morality and law, it appears as a colossal anomaly. Being a self-justified and self-sufficient society, the conspiracy could be viewed as "alter" society—as a grand anomaly, a public mutant, a political monstrosity, or as an unprecedented and sublime mankind. For that reason the Knight of Conspiratorial Faith appears either as an athlete or as a monster. This Knight, however, can under no circumstances be tried as a criminal, a crook or a plotter in terms of bourgeois morality and values because his/her action does not originate through and is not justified by this morality and values. What guarantees and regulates the conspiratorial action is not to be found here, in the bourgeois world.

The conspirator is not asocial; on the contrary, he/she is strictly socialized but within the terms of this "alter" society. To condemn the conspiratorial society on legal and moral grounds means to conceive it as something which it is not.

Confronting the "Western" look, the conspiratorial society appears as a kind of stockade for insulating conspirators in, that is, a society condemned to be a prison by dint of its very existence. Thus this look develops the image of an inferno. Consequently, any political trial against the communist conspiracy and its agents needs to establish certain extra-moral and extra-legal, certain sacramental prerogatives in order to judge its extra-moral and extra-legal origin. A political tribunal would try not persons and actions but a complete society that has itself created its own code and raison d'être. Such a tribunal will try the conspiracy as a planetary threat, conjuring and proceeding from some pre-legal and pre-moral sacral formula of the world, because in fact the conspiracy's political objective is the world.

### THE POST-CONSPIRATORIAL CONDITION

The collapse of communism was caused by the progressive rigidity of the conspiratorial power and its inability to fulfill the plots it designed. The conspiracy cannot be automatically demobilized right after its historical failure. The change in the public life that followed removed its emblems but not the underground communication and channels of the conspiratorial society. They continue to exist, to operate and seek new effective justification, a new sublime composition of words and bodies. This is because conspiracy is a type of society which is mobilized by conjuring language.

Thus the *national argument* has been revived in Eastern Europe after it was criminalized under communism. The rehabilitation of the national idea during this transition period has inspired a nationalistic obsession based on the former conspiratorial practice of the people's consolidation. Conspiracy as a self-same system has been transformed into a nationalistic confederacy. The "national argument" has been blown out of proportion in post-communist societies because too many conspirators and former "conspiratorial cells" have set about to raise it.

Posing the national argument as a problem solvable outside of or even against Statehood has great appeal. Precisely for that reason it can consolidate all kinds of former conspiratorial interests as forces that are by definition against any state. This is possible because *nationhood* goes beyond, it is perceived as something more, something greater than *statehood*. Instigating the national question can help create an ideologically determined confederacy which abuses the state. The rise of national symbols amplified by professed national interest is a strategic endeavor meant to overcome the communist ideological symbolism, enabling conspiratorial society to evolve into a state of uni-national concord.

Nationalism is a post-conspiratorial condition of society. It demobilizes communist ideology and rehabilitates the conspirators.

### IN FLAGRANTE DELICTO

All this conspiratorial pirouette transforms the territory of the state simulacrum into an immense scene of crime. This is a scene of crime which the criminals can neither leave, nor can they remain there. The entire population inhabiting the utopia is under suspicion.

Who will lead the nation out of the scene of crime?

### THE ANTI-UTOPIA

The virtual anti-utopia is the utopia identified as scene of a crime, as a criminal topos.

When a society chronically reaffirms its being conspiratorial, when the public state perpetuates itself as a scene of crime, the only thing to wait for is Fortinbras to enter and pronounce the words: "Take up the bodies."


# The Constitution of Social Integritas

*Voluntas superior est Intellectu.*

### THE THREE RESOURCES:
### EFFECTIVE / AFFECTIVE EXPENDITURE

Capital, will to power, libido—these are the three constituents of the resource that sustain social integritas.

The mass of the resource and the forms of its activation are the basis of social life. Industrial society through its political and market system, principle of ownership, moral code and regulation of the public and private space organizes the spending of the resource in an effective way. Effective investing and consumption results in a progressive stimulation of the resource, which increases its capacity. The society which makes the resource increase is just. By contrast, affective consumption causes excessive, exulting exhaustion and overexpenditure of the resource. Political, or economic, or sexual affect bursts the floodgates of the resource open. How is the flood to be held under control? Communism demonstrated the technique.

## THE GRAND ACCIDENT

The reality of communism is utterly spectacular: an impeccable monumental assemblage of factories, chimney-stacks, construction sites, parading masses, flying tip-wagons, magic words and slogans, a mausoleum, a Mummy surrounded by the tough figures of the future. That was before the grand accident took place in the system and the subsequent excess whereby the work force, the will to power and the libido in 1989 merged into a revolt of streets and squares. The more complete the merger of the three constituents of the resource, the more the affective regime of its expenditure—permanent erection, mass-orgasm, nationalist excess, ejaculation of masses on the streets. The big accident which communism caused in the economy and public life made resources directly visible, brought back to their ecstatic source and elemental drive.

Marx (on capital), Nietzsche (on the will to power) and Freud (on the libido) developed powerful critical theories and practices to make visible what is otherwise transformed, screened and sublimated in private/public forms of life. Production, power, body and spirit procure and reproduce the mass of the resource. The routine production regime necessitates critical theories shatter the "pictorial reality" and expose the hidden mechanism that guarantees its integrity. However, critical theories lose their ground during the grand accident because the dismantling of the system and laying bare of the social reality becomes immediate. By contrast, this necessitates a story about the accident. A suggestive narrative, a grand device must be composed in order to make the accident happen as ontological catastrophe. The communist accident evokes the figures of a grand narrative rather than critical procedure.

## THE IDIO-SYNCRASY

The construction of social integritas, its macro- and micro-structures, political, economic and private life, segment the nebulous mass of the resource into capital, power and libido. Violation of the law of the segmentation and discrimination of these major parts of the resource threatens society with chaos, collapse or stress, that is, with accident. Communism is a society with a low segmentation of the resource. This enables the radical cohesion and merge of state and party, politics and aesthetics, population and conspiracy, ideology and reality, patriarchal and political structures, family and party allegiance. This syncrasy of resources leads to an excessively exalted communal mode of life.

Communism is a social idiosyncrasy based on a radical merge (*synkrasis*) of resources. The homogenization of the resource was maximized and ceremonies of its utterly affective consumption were inaugurated. The difference between economic and political structures was blurred in the campaigns of ecstatic reality. The party emerged with the state power and thus it swelled as cult object of desire and irrational faith. The worker was a knight, the work process was a hammer-and-sickle crusade.

### AFFECT AND DEFECT

Communism accomplished ultimate exhaustion of the resources: shock workers, labor heroism, feats, Party duty, self-sacrifice, mass "laboroid" exaltations in the construction of towns, canals and tunnels which unite the bodies.

The product was defective but the figure of the Creator—ultimately effective. He crushed and shaped time, land surface and humans. The Party appeals made him yield in sublime affect. The products of affective labor had proved defective. Defective factories, defective machines, defective towns and defective goods aggregated throughout the communist space. This defective reality sublimated in symbolic ceremonies and demonstrations: grandiose marches, parades and mass campaigns, historic congresses, strategic watersheds. Throughout the monumental space the Party operated with a different symbolic equipment of bold metaphors, hammers, sickles and five-pointed stars centered on the mummified Progenitor.

This huge aggregate of defective realities projecting through the vast wasteland of communism was left over by the affect of masses plunged in orgies of symbols and ecstatic services in the face of the Mummy that has consolidated the communist physique of mankind.

The communist affect eventually exhausted the resource which resulted in acute shortage of capital, power and libidinous stimulation, in mass apathy and frigidity. It brought about an economic catastrophe, demographic distress and complete sclerosis of power. The magic word has ceased to work and the social body dissipated.

### SPECTERS HAUNT DEFECTIVE REALITIES

Paranoia is the idiosyncrasy of communism.

Defective reality swell up to catastrophic proportions. The gigantic aggregate of wrecked objects released fearsome visions of mammoth fists crushing down, titanic figures bolting out of the blue like meteors. The frenetic fear of the uttered words overwhelmed the mind.

Ruins are the allegorical devices which generate paranoid visions. The aggregate of ruins is haunted by the specter of communism. He peeks through the cracked reality. The specter could make up for the defect as He grants a magic assignment to it.

The spell of communism dispersed as soon as the resource was exhausted. Affect became impossible and the population continued populating defective realities in apathy and melancholy. Communist idols could no longer organize the collective libido, affection and faith. The Specter withered away. The allegorical aggregate of ruins was desolated.

### INTEGRITAS OF AFFECTIVE DESIRES
### OR STRUCTURED INTERESTS

Communism is a homogenized society that lacks structured economic and political interests. The communist political project forcibly dismantled the bourgeois structure of interests without forming a new one that could last and gratify social life.

The basic drive of the subject who belongs to the communist integritas, as alternative to the capitalist one, is to penetrate and consume the immediate body of power. Communism formed a homogeneous mass actor entirely proletarianized in terms of resources. The paroxysmal vigor of this actor was agitated through the system of Party power, the only master of the resource. Hence, this mass actor had no structured interest while performing the grandiose affective economy of communism.

Capital, will to power and libido were usurped by the center of the system. The General Secretary generalized the entire resource. He was the idol and the conjurer of the social spell. He procured the resource and was its organ of excitement. The subjects were prompt to invest or to give up all their will to power, libido and labor force to this Organ.

The Head Party Organ was veiled in a conspiratorial incognito which utterly increased its erotic constitution and potency. This Organ was desired like a formidable phallic creature. The Party patriarchal structure developed extreme phallocratic and erectionist system of signification and organization of desire.

A society based on formalized interest and politics of mediation and segmentation of the resource disintegrated through the Revolution into a society of mass affectation—labor feats, chanting conjuring slogans and total submission to the Mummy. Where interests disintegrate into affects, there the state becomes obsolete and expires. A tough hand stimulates and holds on the permanent mass affectation. So, the integritas of interests is the reverse of the integritas of affects.

### THE NATIONAL AFFECT

The postcommunist situation imperils social integrity. Power disintegrates and a new formula of people's togetherness is to be enforced. Nationalism comes to induce a new maximum of the collective affect and ecstasy. It stages the "genuine national interest" and thus pulls society together by force of a naturalized element rather than legal contract. Nationalism consolidates society by virtue of new ideological devices. It excites the national organism and instinct for expansion and geopolitical reconstitution rather than implementing universal law, human rights and common sense. The disenchantment with communist ideological integrity spawns nationalism as a relapse which can hold society passionately together prior to the establishment of any state, constitution, law and economic interest.

### THE END MATERALIZED

What is under way with a striking clarity is the end of the social integritas called communism. The end is materialized: catastrophe, distress, paroxysmal nations, incrimination on a mass scale. The scene of crime confines the criminal and the corpse together.

The matter of the end is the only resource. The beginning is projected on the screen of the end. In the beginning was the end.


## THE DANGEROUS INTELLECT

*danger is an opium for the brave.*
          *V. Todorov*

## THE JOB ABSCESS

*So went Satan forth from the presence of the Lord and
smote Job with sore boils from the sole of his foot unto
his crown. Then crept Job upon the dunghill in the outskirts of the town and squatted down into the slops.
And he took him a sharp piece of stone from the ruins
to scrape his pus and scabs withal, his inflamed body to
scratch open, his itch to cure through pain, to coin arro-
gant words out of his moans and turn himself into a
dangerous monster.*
*Adapted from the Book of Job, ii. 7, 8*

## THE INTELLECT AND THE SIMULATOR

Communism has been scientifically proven. This was the undefeatable
argument in favor of its existence. Agit-prop became the school of revolutionary arts and sciences. It was gradually evolved into a system of
universities, academies, theaters, and party cells for enlightenment of
the population. Agit-prop intellect (analytical and artistic) was appointed to provide the proofs and the images of the communist world
and thus to enhance its categorical clarity and transparency.

Any manifestation of vagueness or opacity faced correction. Vagueness was the gravest danger because it bears monstrosity. So many
works of art were amputated on the simple basis of being vague. Vagueness enhances the ambiguity of meaning and the claim for a special
spirituality and uniqueness which was considered outrageous.

The aesthetic extremities were wasted as dangerous pollution of
public life. The communist enlightenment launched series of sanitation
campaigns against the eccentric aestheticism through isolation and concentration of its actors in a special dump.

The end of communism found the intellect either as a cynical
schoolmaster who faced the end of the textbook and became extinct,
or as a Job who, reddened with sores, festers in exile in obscene words
and vulgar postures and drags his body amid the ruins of the withered
Revolution.

During the hegemony of the Red doctrine most of the intelligentsia
was centralized and concentrated within the power because this was
the author and herald of the New World. Words were charged with immense ideological power. Whoever coined and guarded words was initiated into the secrets of power. The Red doctrine was characterized by
a surplus-production of words and visions, not a production of commodities. The syntagmata of language created reality. Magic words

manufactured communism. One could carry out only what one could utter in the presence of power. And only that which was enunciated by authority could occur, nothing else. The appearance of anything that differed from the Party word was repressed as subversive. Stalin's physicians could treat him only according to a diagnosis they dared pronounce in his presence.

The communist ideology was a lurid simulator which trained reality to exist correctly. Intellect was incessantly revising, arranging and assembling anew the syntagmata of the simulator, readjusting thereby the communist instruction of the population.

### WRITING AS CLAIM FOR POWER

The system of communism gave creative writing a crucial ideological assignment. The system itself had the appearance of a magnum opus created by a political genius which accommodated and disciplined the entire social body under the code of an all-embracing ideology. The radical concept that postulated state authority as an author of a magnum opus molded the image of the artist, his/her public accomplishments and political commitment. Creative writing was considered an exceptional act that resembles and thus testifies to the otherwise unfathomable process of system formation and elaboration. Writers create miniatures of the system and thus the act of writing acquired the political determination of statesmanship. The principle of communist ideology was: aesthetics renders politics visible.

Creative writing performed the state principle and contributes to the total performance carried out by the genius of the Party patron. Apparently the party Patron Kim Il Sung has good reason to endorse the grand Korean operas as their ultimate author. Any other "name" with claims to authorship would claim in fact His power.

Authors who resisted inside the system were judged as people who claimed power. This demarcated them from those critics of the system who had escaped it. That is precisely why dissidents and not emigrants had the ontological status to represent the body of the new power after the collapse of the system. Communism inaugurated and canonized the sublime *inside presence* and visibility of those who did not desert it. This marked the great *geopolitical difference* between the resistance of an insider and that of an outsider in Eastern Europe. The geopolitical position of a writer determines his/her achievement and right to partake in power. We could illustrate this by mentioning the Havel/Kundera juxtaposition as a perfect example for two different politics of writing which map the *geopolitical difference* in terms of the writer's presence.

The virtual difference made by Kundera's writing is determined by the Western book market and not by a national body engaged in carrying out communism. An author who existed outside the grand work of the system could be its critic, but nothing more radical. Conversely, a dissident writer claimed power by writing inside it.

Writing legitimizes power—this principle of communism still operates in the transitional period. Writers shared in the power because communism made them claim power. This was the primal determination of writing. Writers have taken power during the transition period in order to reconfirm and reaffirm their crucial public relevance and thus to revalidate their mission in a changing society. A major intuition still works—writing outside the realm of power can only be a bourgeois occupation or a marginal extravagance.

Writers have become again the statesmen of change. For they can forge a state out of new words! Nevertheless, we must carefully acknowledge that democracy demands different governing qualifications and poets get gradually disqualified. The spell of Letters has been broken and the state doomed to "wither away" has been dismantled. Writers experience today a surge of nostalgia toward the lost spellbinding power of writing.

### INTELLIGENTSIA AND AUTHORIZATION

The messianic mien of the Russian intelligentsia was shaped over the last two centuries. A special learned community was assembled to bear and secure society's "true values" against changing political systems and forms of power. This community set about the mission to speak for the "speechless" people; however, it has always been split between its "conservative" and "democratic" wings, and its consolidation has always failed.

The intelligentsia develops a strategic consciousness with a clearly formulated perspective. It professes a universal code and worldview, lives and dies for ideas. Intelligentsia launches public campaigns and debates, defeating or promoting certain value systems. It constantly endeavors to raise and sustain the correct self-consciousness and political awareness of the nation. The justification of this community consists of three major, ever debated claims to existence: a *mission* with a conceptual *end;* a *vision* of the ultimate *objective;* and a *manifestation* of universal *intelligence.* The intellect erected upon these three sacred columns becomes a mighty public actor that claims ultimate political knowledge and responsibility. These three claims are publicly enforced through a *categorical self-authorization* of the intelligentsia as prophet, redeemer and scapegoat in one body incarnate. The intelligentsia is a collective body that endeavors to acquire and expand universal knowledge and decorum. This body testifies to the existence of truth. It is a self-authorized embodiment of truth.

Communism magnified the status of intellectuals. The intelligentsia was recruited to saturate the entire public space with suggestive visions, to enact the correct thinking, and to handle current public debates. The major problem of the intelligentsia under communism was that it ceased to be a self-authorized community, being granted authority by the Party ruler. Under communism the Party itself represents the only possible self-authorized power. We confront here a special problem. The Communist Party was originally established by the so-called revolutionary intelligentsia and later gained the most real and ultimate self-authorization by expropriating the instrument of political power itself. The Party took over society through ideologically self-authorized (revolutionary) appropriation of power and forceful replacement of state institutions during the notorious proletarian dictatorship—a violent form of political self-authorization whereby the Party claimed the right to exterminate agents of the old world.

The case of the communist intelligentsia is a special one because communism was initially proclaimed as a scientifically proven and creatively determined society that mobilizes the entire intellect to its elaboration. The intelligentsia ceased to be a self-authorized body endowed with an autonomous mission, vision and intelligence, administrated by no government, state apparatus, or procedures for legitimate public promotion. Communism itself turned to be a blatant self-authorization of the radical scientific and creative intellect.

## The Infinite Parable

Divine Intelligence plots so that the Messiah encounters the Procurator and a sudden scene of recognition takes place: "Who are you?,"—asks Pilate. "I have come into the world to testify to the Truth," says Jesus. "What is Truth?," asks Pilate, then exits the stage and leaves the question demonstratively hanging. The Messiah remains unrecognized. His testimony is left radiating in the void.

It is a common judgment that the Procurator takes no responsibility. He exercises institutionalized competence that ultimately discards Truth and its incarnates. The Procurator takes no blame for the authority he represents excuses the deeds of the person he is. Conversely, the Messiah manifests a self-authorized knowledge that cannot be disproved. For his knowledge is not a matter of competence, but manifestation of Truth. He is the enforcer of the divine Intelligence. The Messiah is a figure that manifests and not a person that represents authority. He needs no recognition. He knows no remorse. But he is doomed to bear his radical incognito against the ever looming Revelation. The most that man can do is to wash his feet and follow him. Man happens to wash either Messiah's feet or his hands.

When the Messiah enters the stage, the Procurator instantly poses two ultimate questions that cut Messiah to the quick—"Who are you?" and "What is Truth?" Immediately after this, the Procurator leaves the stage for he cannot handle the Messiah's presence. For he has indeed recognized Him. Silent, the Procurator leaves to wash his hands. And people rush onto the stage to take the blame while shouting—"Crucify him! Crucify him! Crucify him!"

### ALCHEMY OF DECAY AND RUINISM

The post-communist prophets hone their sharp ironies, herald the coming of doomsday, draw apocalyptic visions. Groans to high heaven and the stench of rotting flesh infect society.

The aestheticization of decay is affected to foist on us the image of the ruins and in this way move us deeply and strike us by tragic shock. Prophets are dragging the chains of the former exile and exposing the festering sores of anguish. Other impostors act as Lot, Ahasuerus, Job and Onan.

The new prophet drags along papier-maché ruins. The prophet maximizes a trauma, waves about prosthesis, twists insolent sentences and imposes a new aesthetic authoritarianism conjured up to shock the world. The prophet demonstrates striking figures on a trapeze assembled out of ruins. Thus man marks the End.

### DER WILLE ZUM MESSIAS

*Die Wuste wachst.*
*Nietzsche*

The Party Patron protruding on the center of communism was ripped out. The center gapes as a bleeding uterus. People expect a Messiah to appear out of the wound and to head for the zone where the maximum aesthetisization of defects, decay and collapse demonstrates, the zone where the space is fraught gangrene and crippled creatures, the zone where all charlatans and fakes have flocked.

The Messiah always appears on the boundary between the ruined city and the desert, at the place where the desert swallows up the ruins and swells, where the social order is limited by the wasteland.

The Messiah comes to check the surge of the desert and to lead the impostors out of it. He is the buffer between the ruins and the onrushing sands.

Ubu-Roi will appear amid the ruins and will shout out the word he always shouts at the very Beginning of the political ob-scena: Merdre!

Language waits for the Messiah to speak.

### THE IMPREGNATION OF DANGER

The East aestheticizes its monstrosity for the West, its ruins, its fakes, its own end and thus raises the price at which the West pays for the danger because the West has been investing in the thrills of the ruins from the very beginning.

Danger impregnated with money becomes a thriller.

### END

Surrounded by the ruins I feel an exuberant mirth well up in Me. The rotting Job is merry because the Repetition will not take place.

The End

# The Author in the Age
## of the Modernized Imagination

The revolution mocked the Romantic idea of creative genius submerged in a transcendent obscurity.

The idea of the author as power having transcendent originality and arbitrary imagination had undergone a radical political reduction.

The ultimate author is the political authority. The ultimate work is the world.

The new author composes using ready-made figures of speech.

History is possible for political narrative re-collects the ruins.

The political authority possesses the most powerful imagination. It imagines the real.

Public space is power. Bodies are subject in it to perform political mimesis, to conform to the there-installed-paradigms and thus they become social. The political imagination molds a public space where bodies mimetically merge with paradigms.

The aesthetic is the sublime of the political.

The political is aesthetically justified.

Mimetically the body dwells.

# TRA - LA - LA, TRA - LA - LA

## WE THREW OUT THE CRYING BABY IN US

Dada

# REFERENCES


Abalkin, N. 1950. *Sistema Stanislavskogo i sovetskii teatr.* Moscow: Iskusstvo.

Avrich, Paul, ed. 1973. *The Anarchists in the Russian Revolution.* Ithaca: Cornell University Press.

Benjamin, W. "Central Park." *New German Critique* 34 (1985): 32–55.

Bowlt, John, ed. 1988. *Russian Art of the Avant-garde: Theory and Criticism, 1902–1934.* New York: Thames and Hudson.

Braun, Edward, ed. 1969. *Meyerhold on the Theatre.* New York: Hill and Wang.

Brecht, Bertold. 1968. "The Street Scene: A Basic Model for an Epic Theater." *The Theory of the Modern Stage,* ed. Eric Bentley. Harmondsworth: Penguin Books.

Brodskii, N. L., V. L'vov-Rogachevskii, and N. P. Sidorov, eds. 1929. *Literaturnye manifesty: ot simvolizma k oktiabriu.* Moscow: Federatsiia.

Conrads, Ulrich, ed. 1970. *Programs and Manifestoes on 20th-Century Architecture.* Cambridge: MIT Press.

Eisenstein, Sergei. 1964. "Montazh attraktsionov." *Izbranye proizvedeniia v 6-ti tomakh,* vol. 2. Moscow: Iskusstvo.

Elagin, Yuri. 1982. *Temnyi genii.* London: Overseas Publications Interchange Ltd.

Ermolaev, Herman. 1977. *Soviet Literary Theories: 1917–1934. The Genesis of Socialist Realism.* New York: Ostagon Books.

Evreinov, Nikolai. 1976. "The Fourth Wall." *Russkaia teatralnaia parodiia XIX—nachala XX veka.* Moscow: Iskusstvo.

Fyodorov, Nikolai. 1982. *Sochineniia.* Moscow: Mysl'.

Gastev, Aleksei. 1971. *Poeziia rabochego udara.* Moscow: Khudozhest-
vennaia literatura.

Goethe, J. W. 1952. *Goethe's Botanical Writings,* trans. B. Mueller. Hon-
olulu: University of Hawaii Press.

Golub, Spencer. 1984. *Evreinov: The Theatre of Paradox and Transformation.*
Ann Arbor: UMI.

Gorchakov, Nikolai. 1957. *The Theater in Soviet Russia,* trans. Edgar
Lehrman. New York: Columbia University Press.

Gorkii, Maksim. 1980. "Speech at the First All-Union Convention of Soviet Writers, 17 August 1934." *Preobrazhenie mira.* Moscow: Sovet-
skaia Rossia.

*Hippocratic Writings.* 1978. G. Lloyd Harmondsworth, ed. Penguin Books.

Ch. Joachimides, and N. Rosenthal, and W. Schmied, eds. 1985. *German
Art in the 20th Century: Painting and Sculpture 1905–1985.* Munich:
Prastel-Verlag.

Huelsenbeck, Richard. 1920. *En Avant Dada: Die Geschichte des Dadais-
mus.* Hanover: Steegmann.

Kafka, Franz. 1966. *Parables and Paradoxes.* New York: Schocken Books.

Kamenskii, Vasilii. 1940. *Zhisn' s Maiakovskim.* Moscow: Khudo-
zhestvennaia Literatura.

Kierkegaard, Soren. 1983. *Fear and Trembling,* eds. Howard Hong and
Edna Hong. Princeton: Princeton University Press.

Kopp, Anatole. 1970. *Town and Revolution.* New York: George Braziller.

Kuenzli, Rudolf. ed. 1986. *New York Dada.* New York: Willis Locker &
Owens.

Lawton, Anna, ed. 1988. *Russian Futurism Through its Manifestoes,
1912–1928.* Ithaca: Cornell University Press.

*LEF AGITKI: Agit-zametki A. Kruchenykh.* 1925. Moscow: Izdanie Vserossiiskogo Soiuza Poetov.

Lenin, Vladimir. 1980. "Partiinaia organizatsiia i partiinaia literatura." *Iz istorii Sovetskoi esteticheskoi mysli; 1917–1932,* eds. G. A. Belaia and A. E. Gorpenko. Moscow: Iskusstvo.

Lenin, Vladimir. 1966. "What is to be Done." *Essential Works of Lenin,* ed. H. M. Christman. New York: Bantam Books.

Lissitzky, El. 1970. *Russia: An Architecture of World Revolution,* trans. Eric Dluhosch. Cambridge, Mass.: MIT Press.

Mandelstam, Osip. 1987. *Slovo i kul'tura.* Moscow: Sovetskii Pisatel'.

Motherwell, R. and J. Flam, eds. 1986. *The Duda Painters and Poets: An Anthology.* Boston: G. K. Hall and Co.

Krupskaia, Nadezhda. 1980. "Proletarskaia Ideologiia i Proletkul't." *Iz istorii Sovetskoi esteticheskoi mysli 1917–1932.* Moscow: Iskusstvo.

Platonov, Andrei. 1973. *The Foundation Pit—Kotlovan: A Bi-lingual Edition.* Ann Arbor: Ardis Publishers.

Platonov, Andrei. 1989. "Slyshnye shagi: revoliutsia i matematika." *Vozvrashchenie.* Moscow: Molodaia Gvardiia.

Reich, Wilhelm. 1960. *Selected Writings.* New York: Farrar, Straus & Cudahy.

Reich, Wilhelm. 1972. *SEX-POL: Essays 1929–1934,* ed. Lee Baxandall. New York: Vintage Books.

Rozanov, Vasilii. 1978. *Four Faces of Rozanov: Christianity, Sex, Jews and the Russian Revolution,* ed. Spencer Roberts. New York: Philosophical Library.

Rudnitsky, Konstantin. 1981. *Meyerhold: The Director,* transl. G. Petrov. Ann Arbor: Ardis.

S-kii, N. A. 1934. "O smerti i pogrebenii." *Vselenskoe Delo* 2 (1934): 141–46.

Seliger, Martin. 1977. *The Marxist Conception of Ideology.* London: Cambridge University Press.

Shklovskii, Viktor. 1980. "Iskusstvo kak priem." *Iz istorii Sovetskoi esteticheskoi mysli: 1917–1932,* ed. G. A. Belaia and A. E. Gorpenko. Moscow: Iskusstvo.

Stanislavskii, Konstantin. 1961. *Creating a Role,* ed. Hermine Popper. New York: Theater Arts Books.

Starr, Frederick. 1978. *Melnikov: Solo Architect in a Mass Society.* Princeton University Press.

Stephan, Halina. 1981. *LEF and the Left Front of the Arts.* Munich: Verlag Otto Sagner.

Sternberg, Hilary, and Lydia Bott, trans. 1974. *Daughter of a Revolutionary: Natalie Herzen and the Bakunin-Nechayev Circle,* ed. Michael Confino. London: Alcove Press.

Struik, D., ed. 1971. *Birth of the Communist Manifesto.* New York: International Publishers.

Trifonov, N. A., ed. 1987. *Russkaia literatura XX veka: khrestomatiia.* Moscow: Prosveshchenie.

Tumarkin, Nina. 1983. *LENIN LIVES! The Lenin Cult in Soviet Russia.* Harvard University Press.

Tynianov, Iurii. 1929. "Dostoevskii i Gogol': k teorii parodii." *Arkhaisty i novatory.* Leningrad: Priboi.

Vasil'ev, Vladimir. 1982. *Andrei Platonov: Ocherk zhizni i tvorchestva.* Moscow: Sovremennik.

Vertov, Dziga. 1984. *Kino-Eye: The Writings of Dziga Vertov,* ed. Annette Michelson. Berkeley: University of California Press.

Voloshinov, V. N. 1930. *Marksizm i filosofiia iazyka,* 2nd ed. Leningrad: Priboi.

Voloshinov, V. N. 1983. *Freidizm, Kriticheskii ocherk.* New York: Chalidze Publications. Chapter IX: "Soderzhanie soznaniia kak ideologiia" (The Content of Consciousness as Ideology), sections 3 and 4.

*Vselenskoe Delo* 2 (1934): 113–15.

Wulbern, Julian. 1971. *Brecht and Ionesco.* Urbana: University of Illinois
    Press.

# INDEX